도전! OPIc IM+

CARROT HOUSE

OPIc 도전! IM+
ⓒ Carrot House

All rights reserved. No part of this publication may be reproduced,
stored in a retrieval system, or transmitted in any form or by any means
without the prior permission in writing of Carrot House

Author: Carrot Language Research & Development, Canada

ISBN 978-89-6732-248-9

Printed and distributed in Korea
9F, 488 Gangnam St., Gangnam-gu, Seoul 06210, Korea

Curriculum Map

Course	Level 1	Level 2	Level 3	Level 4	Level 5	Level 6	Level 7
General Conversation	Essential English : Begin Again; Pre Get Up to Speed 1~2	New Get Up to Speed 1	New Get Up to Speed 2	New Get Up to Speed 3	New Get Up to Speed 4		
	Daily Focused English 1	Daily Focused English 2					
Discussion				Active Discussion 1	Active Discussion 2	Dynamic Discussion	
				Chicken Soup Course			
Business Conversation	Pre Business Basics 1	Pre Business Basics 2	Business Basics 1	Business Basics 2	Business Practice 1	Business Practice 2	
Global Biz Workshop				Effective Business Writing Skills (Workbook)			
				Effective Presentation Skills (Workbook)			
					Effective Negotiation Skills (Workbook)		
				Cross-Cultural Training 1~2 (Workbook)			
					Leadership Training Course (Workbook)		
Business Skills				Simple & Clear Technical Writing Skills			
				Effective Business Writing Skills			
				Effective Meeting Skills			
				Effective Presentation Skills			
				Marketing 1 - 2			
On the Job English				Human Resources			
				Accounting and Finance			
				Marketing and Sales			
				Production Management			
				Automotive			
				Banking and Commerce			
				Medical and Medicine			
				Information Technology			
			Construction English in Use 1 ~ 4				
			Public Service English in Use				
TEST Preparation		★ OPIc 도전! IM+			OPIc 공략! IM3+		
				ATEC OPIc			
				How to Say it, Logically?			
		TOEIC Speaking 도전! Level 5					
				TOEIC Speaking 공략! Level 7			

※ This Curriculum Map illustrates the entire line-up of textbooks at CARROT HOUSE.

Introduction

Carrot House Methodology

Andragogical Approach & Productive English

The teaching of children (pedagogy) and the teaching of adults (andragogy) are distinctively different. Pedagogy is akin to training and encourages convergent thinking and rote learning. It is compulsory, centered on the teacher and the imparting of information with minimal control by the learner. Andragogy, by contrast, is about education as freedom. It encourages divergent thinking and active learning. It is voluntary, learner oriented and opens up vistas for continuous learning. Adults need to feel independent and in control of their learning. Therefore, Carrot House curriculum is based on andragogy and is designed to involve learners' participation and engagement by providing more task-based activities and opportunities to frequently interact in the classroom.

People want to achieve communicative competence when they learn other languages. English education in EFL environments has been rather focused on receptive skills of English—listening and reading—which just increases learners' knowledge about language, not the competence of using them. If people are well equipped with productive skills—speaking and writing—they will be competent in English communication. This is why Carrot House curriculum is designed to enhance learners' productive skills throughout the course. This andragogical approach of the Carrot House Curriculum, which focuses on productive English, will enable learners to achieve communication skills necessary for global competence. Carrot House's teaching philosophy and curriculum combined pursues a "Language for Success" for all learners.

Communicative Language Learning (CLL)

This communicative interaction, the essential component of language acquisition, does not occur in a typical, non-meaningful, fun-oriented conversation with native speakers. It occurs in a negotiated interaction through which a well-trained teacher provides comprehensible input that is appropriate to the learners. The learners actively utilize the opportunities given to them by the teachers.

To this end, the Communicative Language Learning (CLL) method is employed in the field of Foreign Language Acquisition. CLL provides the activities that are geared toward using language pragmatically, authentically and functionally with the intention of achieving meaningful purposes.

목 차

OPIc 도전! IM+

I. OPIc 이해하기
- OPIc 이란? — 10
- Background Survey — 14
- OPIc FAQ — 16

II. 실력 다지기

Part 1 공통질문
- Unit 1. 자기소개 — 21
- Unit 2. 인물 묘사 — 27
- Unit 3. 장소 묘사 — 33

Part 2 설문주제

Category 1 일상생활
- Unit 4. 직장생활 — 41

Category 2 여가활동
- Unit 5. 영화보기 — 47
- Unit 6. 카페가기 — 53
- Unit 7. 바/펍 가기 — 59
- Unit 8. 공원가기 — 65
- Unit 9. 해변가기 — 71

Category 3 취미와 관심사
- Unit 10. 음악 감상하기 — 77

Category 4 운동
- Unit 11. 조깅/걷기 — 83

Category 5 휴가
- Unit 12. 국내 여행 — 89
- Unit 13. 해외 여행 — 95
- Unit 14. 집에서 보내는 휴가 — 101

Part 3 롤플레이
- Unit 15. Eva에게 질문하기 — 109
- Unit 16. 전화로 질문하기 — 115
- Unit 17. 상황 설명하기 — 121
- Unit 18. 대안 제시하기 — 127

Part 4 돌발주제
- Unit 19. 집안일 — 135
- Unit 20. 외식 — 141
- Unit 21. 재활용 — 147
- Unit 22. 계절 — 153
- Unit 23. 약속 — 159
- Unit 24. 쇼핑 — 165

III. 실전 OPIc
- Actual Test 1 — 172
- Actual Test 2 — 174

IV. 부록
- IM-IH 학습가이드
- OPIc 가이드 라인
- OPIc 금지답변

교재구성 알아보기

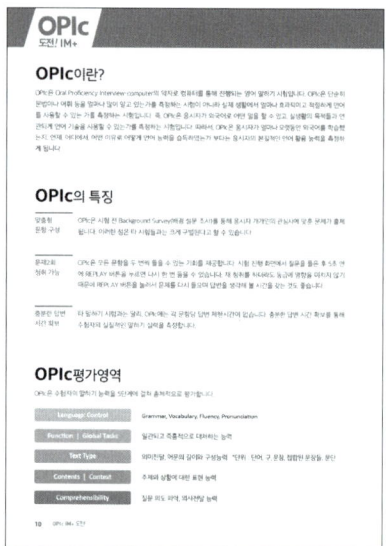

01 OPIc 이해하기

오픽 시험의 구성과 특징 및 평가영역에 대해 알아봅니다.

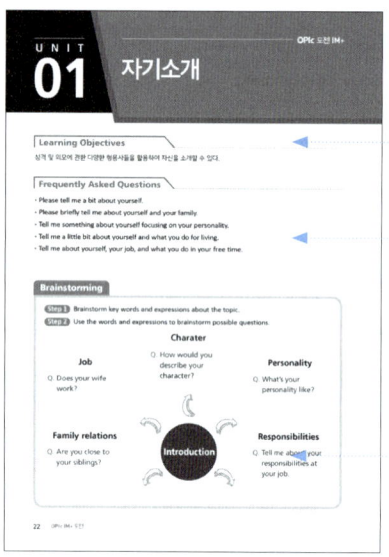

02 실력 다지기

Learning Objective
각 Unit의 학습목표가 제시됩니다.

Frequently Asked Questions
자주 출제되고 있는 질문을 미리 살펴봄으로써 주제별 질문유형을 이해하고 해당 학습내용을 파악합니다.

Brainstorming
학습자 수준에 따라 Brainstorming은 다음과 같이 진행됩니다.

 주제별 필수 어휘 및 표현을 브레인스토밍 합니다.

 브레인스토밍한 어휘 및 표현을 활용해 예상 질문을 만들어 봅니다.

Skill up! Patterns

답변을 할 때 유용하게 사용할 수 있는 표현 패턴을 살펴봅니다.

- 샘플 문장을 통해 자신의 문장을 생각해 봅니다.
- 항목별로 작성된 문장을 배열하면 주제별 답변이 구성됩니다.

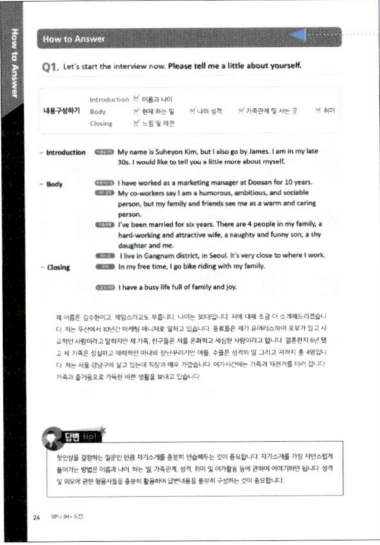

How To Answer

출제가능성이 높은 질문에 대하여 답변 전략을 살펴봅니다.

1. 내용구성하기

답변구성에 필요한 내용을 살펴볼 수 있습니다.

2. Sample Answer

비법노트를 참고하여 보다 효과적인 답변 구성 전략을 파악합니다.

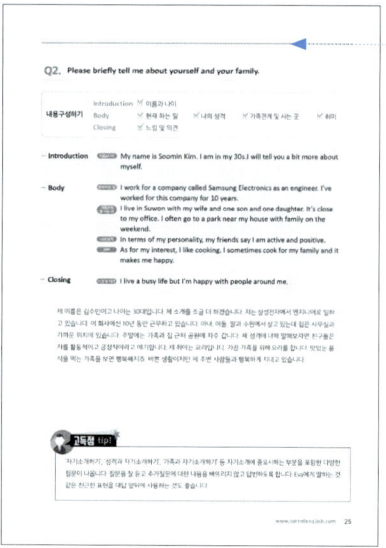

답변 Tip! & 고득점 Tip!
주제별 답변을 쉽게 구성하고 고득점을 받을 수 있는 유익한 정보를 알아봅니다.

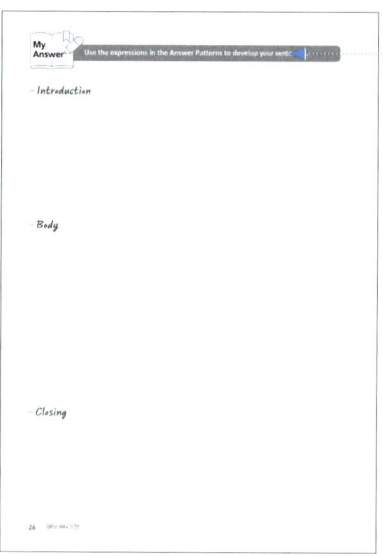

My Answer
앞서 학습한 patterns를 활용해 본인의 답변을 구성할 수 있습니다.

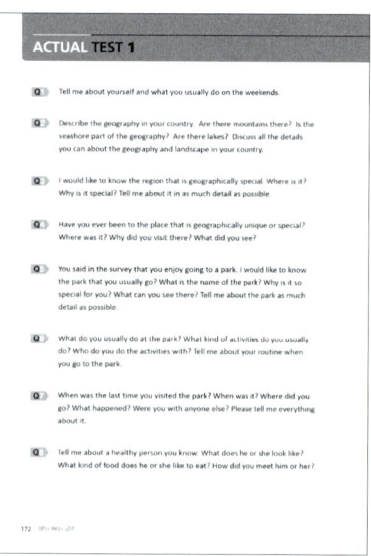

03 실전 OPIc
Actual Test 를 통해 실전감각을 키워 시험 준비를 마무리합니다.

* Actual Test는 MP3파일을 다운로드 받아 활용하시기 바랍니다.

I

OPIc 이해하기

- ☑ OPIc 이란?
- ☑ Background Survey
- ☑ OPIc FAQ

OPIc이란?

OPIc은 Oral Proficiency Interview-computer의 약자로 컴퓨터를 통해 진행되는 영어 말하기 시험입니다. OPIc은 단순히 문법이나 어휘 등을 얼마나 많이 알고 있는가를 측정하는 시험이 아니라 실제 생활에서 얼마나 효과적이고 적절하게 언어를 사용할 수 있는 가를 측정하는 시험입니다. 즉, OPIc은 응시자가 외국어로 어떤 일을 할 수 있고, 실생활의 목적들과 연관되게 언어 기술을 사용할 수 있는가를 측정하는 시험입니다. 따라서, OPIc은 응시자가 얼마나 오랫동안 외국어를 학습했는지, 언제, 어디에서, 어떤 이유로 어떻게 언어 능력을 습득하였는가 보다는 응시자의 본질적인 언어 활용 능력을 측정하게 됩니다.

OPIc의 특징

맞춤형 문항 구성
OPIc은 시험 전 Background Survey(배경 설문 조사)를 통해 응시자 개개인의 관심사에 맞춘 문제가 출제됩니다. 이러한 점은 타 시험들과는 크게 구별된다고 할 수 있습니다.

문제2회 청취 가능
OPIc은 모든 문항을 두 번씩 들을 수 있는 기회를 제공합니다. 시험 진행 화면에서 질문을 들은 후 5초 안에 REPLAY 버튼을 누르면 다시 한 번 들을 수 있습니다. 재 청취를 하더라도 등급에 영향을 미치지 않기 때문에 REPLAY 버튼을 눌러서 문제를 다시 들으며 답변을 생각해 볼 시간을 갖는 것도 좋습니다.

충분한 답변 시간 확보
타 말하기 시험과는 달리, OPIc에는 각 문항당 답변 제한시간이 없습니다. 충분한 답변 시간 확보를 통해 수험자의 실질적인 말하기 실력을 측정합니다.

OPIc평가영역

OPIc은 수험자의 말하기 능력을 5단계에 걸쳐 총체적으로 평가합니다.

Language Control	Grammar, Vocabulary, Fluency, Pronunciation
Function ｜ Global Tasks	일관되고 즉흥적으로 대처하는 능력
Text Type	의미전달, 어문의 길이와 구성능력　*단위 : 단어, 구, 문장, 접합된 문장들, 문단
Contents ｜ Context	주제와 상황에 대한 표현 능력
Comprehensibility	질문 의도 파악, 의사전달 능력

OPIc시험 진행 및 유형

시험진행구성

오리엔테이션 (약 20분)
① Background Survey — 시험 문항 출제를 위한 사전 설문
② Self Assessment — 시험 난이도 결정을 위한 자가 평가
③ Overview of OPIc — 화면 구성, 문항 청취 및 답변 방법 안내
④ Sample Question — 실제 답변 방법 연습

본 시험 (약 40분)
① 1st Session — 개인별 맞춤 문항 (질문 청취 2회 가능)
② 난이도 재조정 — 2차 Self Assessment (쉬운 질문, 비슷한 질문, 어려운 질문 중 택1)
③ 2nd Session — 1st와 동일

평가 및 통보
① 답변전송 — 인터넷을 통한 실시간 답변 전송
② 평가 — ACTFL 공인 Rater 신뢰도, 객관성 유지
③ 결과 통보 — 근무일 기준 5일 내외의 신속한 평가 결과 통보

시험 문제 유형

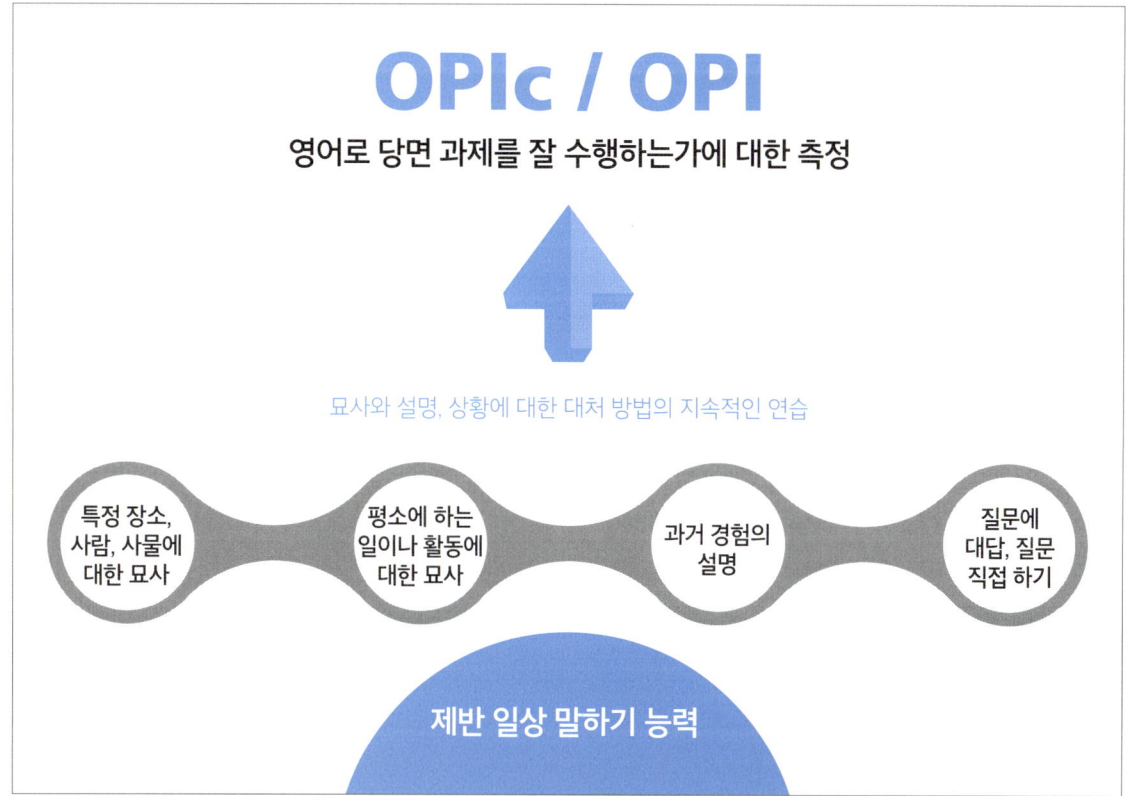

시험 응시화면

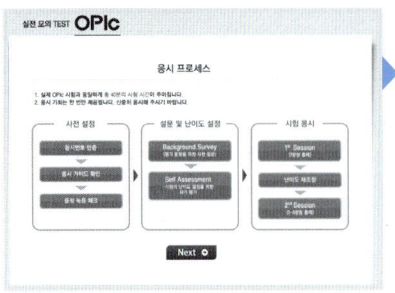

Introduction
시험 전 응시 프로세스가 제시됩니다.

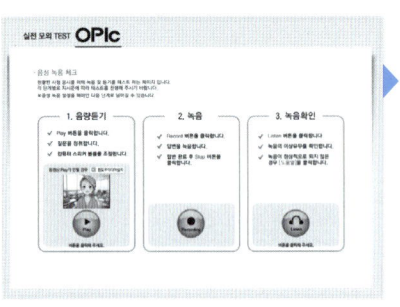

컴퓨터 설정
녹음 및 듣기 테스트를 통해 컴퓨터 환경을 설정합니다.

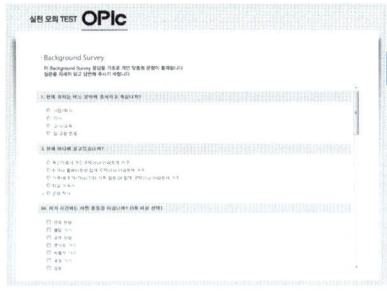

Background Survey
시험 전 Background Survey를 통해 응시자 개개인의 관심사에 맞춘 문제가 출제됩니다.

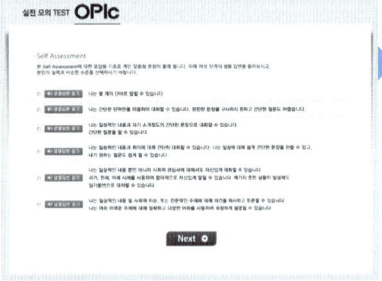

Self Assessment
6가지 등급의 설명을 읽고 각 등급의 샘플 답변을 들은 후 자기 실력에 맞는 등급(1~6등급)을 선택할 수 있습니다.

응시화면 가이드
응시화면 구성을 살펴봅니다. 시험 중 질문을 들은 후 5초안에 play 버튼을 클릭하면 질문을 새정취할 수 있습니다. 답변을 마친 후 Next 버튼을 클릭하면 다음 질문으로 넘어갑니다.

OPIc등급 체계

OPIc의 모체인 OPI에서는 Advanced도 Low, Mid, High로 구분되지만, 컴퓨터로 시험을 보는 OPIc에서는 Advanced Low 라는 등급 하나만 부여됩니다.

Level	레벨별 요약설명
AL (Advanced Low)	다양한 사회적, 학술적 혹은 전문적 주제에 대한 요약문, 일상적인 서신을 능숙하게 작성할 수 있다. 적절한 시제를 활용함은 물론 복잡한 문장구조도 활용하여 다양한 문단 및 단락을 구성하며 글의 내용은 대부분의 원어민들이 쉽게 이해할 수 있다.
IH (Intermediate High)	직장이나 학교에서 필요로 하는 과제에 대하여 다양한 글쓰기가 가능하다. 현재시제 외 기타시제도 활용하지만 약간의 오류를 범하기도 한다. 아이디어를 구성할 수 있고 친숙한 주제 혹은 사건에 관하여 묘사는 물론 요약 및 서술도 가능하다. 글의 내용은 대부분의 원어민들이 이해할 수 있다.
IM (Intermediate Mid)	직장이나 학교에서 필요로 하는 기본적인 글쓰기가 가능하다. 간단한 요약문을 작성 할 수 있고 일상적인 업무와 관련된 서신을 주고 받을 수 있다. 다양한 문장으로 구성된 문단을 작성할 수 있으며, 현재시제 외 기타시제도 가끔은 정확하게 활용할 수 있다. 글의 주요 내용은 대부분의 원어민들이 이해할 수 있다.
IL (Intermediate Low)	친숙한 소재에 관하여 간단한 의견이나 질문 내용을 작성할 수 있다. 주로 현재시제를 활용하지만, 주어-동사-목적어 구조로 활용하여 간단한 의견교환은 할 수 있다.
NH (Novice High)	간단한 단어나 어구를 활용하여 기본적인 작문을 할 수 있다. 어휘 및 문법에 대한 이해 부족으로 인하여 작성한 글이 원어민에 의해 부분적으로만 이해할 수 있다. 친숙한 소재에 관하여 짧은 메시지, 엽서, 리스트 등을 작성할 수 있다.
NM (Novice Mid)	이미 암기한 친숙한 단어나 구를 활용할 수 있다.
NL (Novice Low)	매우 제한적으로 몇몇 단어 및 구를 나열할 수 있다.

BACKGROUND SURVEY

이 Background Survey 응답을 기초로 개인 맞춤형 문항이 출제 됩니다.
질문을 자세히 읽고 답변해 주시기 바랍니다.

1. 현재 귀하는 어느 분야에 종사하고 계십니까?

☐ 사업/회사
☐ 자택근무/재택사업
☐ 교사/교육자
☐ 군복무
☐ 일 경험 없음

2. 현재 귀하는 학생이십니까?

☐ 네
☐ 아니오

3. 현재 귀하는 어디에 살고 계십니까?

☐ 개인 주택이나 아파트에 거주
☐ 친구나 룸메이트와 함께 주택이나 아파트에서 거주
☐ 가족(배우자/자녀/기타 가족 일원)과 함께 주택이나 아파트에 거주
☐ 학교 기숙사
☐ 군대 막사

아래의 4~7번 문항에서 12개 이상을 선택해 주시기 바랍니다.

4. 귀하의 여가 활동으로 주로 무엇을 하십니까? (두 개 이상 선택)

☐ 쇼핑 하기
☐ TV 시청
☐ 리얼리티 쇼 시청
☐ 영화 보기
☐ 클럽/나이트클럽 가기
☐ 공연 보기
☐ 콘서트 보기
☐ 박물관 가기
☐ 공원 가기
☐ 캠핑하기

☐ 해변 가기
☐ 스포츠 관람
☐ 주거 개선(=집안일 거들기)
☐ 술집/바에 가기
☐ 카페/커피 전문점에 가기
☐ 게임 하기
　 (비디오, 카드, 보드, 휴대폰 등)
☐ 당구치기
☐ 체스 하기
☐ SNS에 글 올리기

☐ 친구들과 문자 대화하기
☐ 시험대비 과정 수강하기
☐ 뉴스를 보거나 듣기
☐ 요리 관련 프로그램 시청하기
☐ 차로 드라이브하기
☐ 스파/마사지샵 가기
☐ 구직 활동하기
☐ 자원 봉사하기

5. 귀하의 취미나 관심사는 무엇입니까? (한 개 이상 선택)

- ☐ 독서
- ☐ 아이에게 책 읽어 주기
- ☐ 음악 감상하기
- ☐ 악기 연주하기
- ☐ 혼자 노래 부르거나 합창하기
- ☐ 춤추기
- ☐ 글쓰기(편지, 단편, 시 등)
- ☐ 그림 그리기
- ☐ 요리하기
- ☐ 애완동물 기르기
- ☐ 주식 투자하기
- ☐ 신문 읽기
- ☐ 여행 관련 잡지나 블로그 읽기
- ☐ 사진 촬영하기

6. 귀하는 주로 어떤 운동을 즐기십니까? (한 개 이상 선택)

- ☐ 농구
- ☐ 야구/소프트볼
- ☐ 축구
- ☐ 미식축구
- ☐ 하키
- ☐ 크리켓
- ☐ 골프
- ☐ 배구
- ☐ 테니스
- ☐ 배드민턴
- ☐ 탁구
- ☐ 수영
- ☐ 자전거
- ☐ 스키/스노보드
- ☐ 아이스 스케이트
- ☐ 조깅
- ☐ 걷기
- ☐ 요가
- ☐ 하이킹/트레킹
- ☐ 낚시
- ☐ 태권도
- ☐ 운동 수영 수강하기
- ☐ 운동을 전혀 하지 않음

7. 귀하는 어떤 휴가나 출장을 다녀온 경험이 있습니까? (한 개 이상 선택)

- ☐ 국내 출장
- ☐ 해외 출장
- ☐ 집에서 보내는 휴가
- ☐ 국내 여행
- ☐ 해외 여행

OPIc FAQ

01 시험 당일 무엇을 준비해야 하나요?

시험 당일에는 규정 신분증(주민등록증, 운전면허증, 기간 만료 전 여권, 공무원증 등)을 반드시 지참해야 합니다. 말하기 시험이기 때문에 필기도구 등은 필요하지 않으며 시험이 진행되는 동안에는 컴퓨터 및 게시판을 통해 시간확인을 할 수 있습니다.

02 시험응시 도중 필기도구를 사용하여 답변을 준비해도 되나요?

OPIc 응시자는 필기도구를 가지고 시험장에 입실할 수 없습니다. 따라서 시험 중에 필기도구를 이용하여 메모 등을 하실 수 없으며, 적발 시 부정행위로 처리되어 OPIc 시험 규정에 따라 향후 시험 응시 기회에 제한을 받습니다.

03 Self Assessment란 무엇인가요?

Self Assessment는 난이도 선택을 일컫습니다. OPIc은 본시험 1차와 본시험 2차로 크게 나뉩니다. 본시험 1차는 시험 전에 선택했던 난이도의 수준에 맞는 문제가 출제되는 것이고, 본시험 2차는 본시험 1차를 치른 후 난이도 재조정에서 새롭게 선택한 난이도에 맞는 문제가 출제됩니다. 난이도 재조정에서는 '쉬운 질문, 비슷한 질문, 어려운 질문'중에서 선택하게 됩니다.

04 시험 보는 중간에 Self Assessment로 레벨을 변경하는 것이 성적에 영향을 미치나요?

처음에 높은 레벨로 시작했다가 중간에 낮은 레벨로 바꾸거나, 그 반대로 낮은 레벨에서 시작해서 높은 레벨로 바꾸는 자체로는 성적이 바뀌지 않습니다. 철저히 주어진 답변에 얼마나 충실하게 답변했는지가 성적을 좌우한다고 보면 됩니다. 그러나, 본인이 영어 실력과 너무 동떨어진 레벨을 선택하는 것은 바람직하지 않습니다.

05 난이도에 따라 문제수가 달라지나요?

OPIc은 Self-Assessment에서 선택한 난이도(총 1~6단계)에 따라 12~15개의 문제가 출제됩니다.

1~2단계에서는 보통 12문제가 출제되고 난이도 초급으로 분류할 수 있습니다. 이 단계에서는 보통 항목당 두 문제 정도가 출제되고 문제 빠르기와 난이도가 비슷하다고 할 수 있습니다.

3~4단계에서는 15문제가 출제되며 난이도 중급으로 이해할 수 있습니다. 3단계와 4단계의 난이도는 큰 차이가 없으므로 IL~IM등급을 준비하고 있다면 3~4단계를 선택하면 됩니다.
3단계 이상부터는 항목당 세 문제, 즉 Three Combo 문제가 등장하게 됩니다.

5~6단계 역시 15문제가 출제되며 난이도는 고급에 해당됩니다. 최고 난이도답게 3~4단계 수준의 문제 이외에 다소 어려운 시사 관련 문제가 등장합니다. 따라서 초·중·고급 난이도의 차이점을 정확하게 이해하고 선택하는 것이 중요합니다.

06 Background Survey 내용과 관련이 없는 문제도 출제되나요?

OPIc은 Background Survey를 통해 수험자의 개인 맞춤형 문항출제가 가능하지만 다른 영역의 질문 또한 출제되어 수험자가 예상하지 못한 문제에 대한 상황 대처능력 및 순발력 또한 평가합니다. 따라서, Background Survey에서 선택한 내용과 다른 문제가 출제되더라도 최선을 다해 성실하게 답변하는 것이 좋습니다.

07 문제를 반복해서 들으면 성적에 안 좋은 영향을 미치나요?

문제를 반복 청취하는 것이 성적에 직접적으로 영향을 미치는 것은 아닙니다. 하지만 문제를 반복 청취했을 때 답변 시간이 줄어들 수밖에 없으므로, 시간 관리에 어려움을 느낄 수도 있습니다. OPIc 문제의 답변 시간은 질문 청취 시간을 제외하고 약 35분 가량입니다. 따라서 주어진 시간 내 모든 문제에 효율적으로 답변할 수 있도록 시간을 활용해야 합니다.

08 성적이 UR이라고 나오는 것은 무엇을 의미하나요?

"UR"은 unable to rate을 의미합니다. UR은 녹음 불량, 녹음 음량이 너무 작은 경우, 수험자가 답변을 하지 않은 경우에 해당합니다. 수험자의 과실인 경우 응시료 환불 및 재시험의 기회가 주어지지 않습니다. 반면, 시스템적인 오류로 UR이 나왔을 경우 한 번의 재시험 기회를 드립니다.

OPIc
도전!
IM+

실력다지기

☑ **Part 1 공통질문**

Unit 1 | 자기소개
Unit 2 | 인물 묘사
Unit 3 | 장소 묘사

It is difficult to say what is impossible,
for the dream of yesterday is the hope of today and the reality of tomorrow.

불가능이 무엇인가는 말하기 어렵다.
어제의 꿈은 오늘의 희망이며 내일의 현실이기 때문이다.
- 로버트 고다드 (*Robert H. Goddard*) -

OPIc
도전! IM+

UNIT 1

자기소개

UNIT 01 자기소개

Learning Objectives

성격 및 외모에 관한 다양한 형용사들을 활용하여 자신을 소개할 수 있다.

Frequently Asked Questions

- Please tell me a bit about yourself.
- Please briefly tell me about yourself and your family.
- Tell me something about yourself focusing on your personality.
- Tell me a little bit about yourself and what you do for a living.
- Tell me about yourself, your job, and what you do in your free time.

Brainstorming

Step 1 Brainstorm key words and expressions about the topic.
Step 2 Use the words and expressions to brainstorm possible questions.

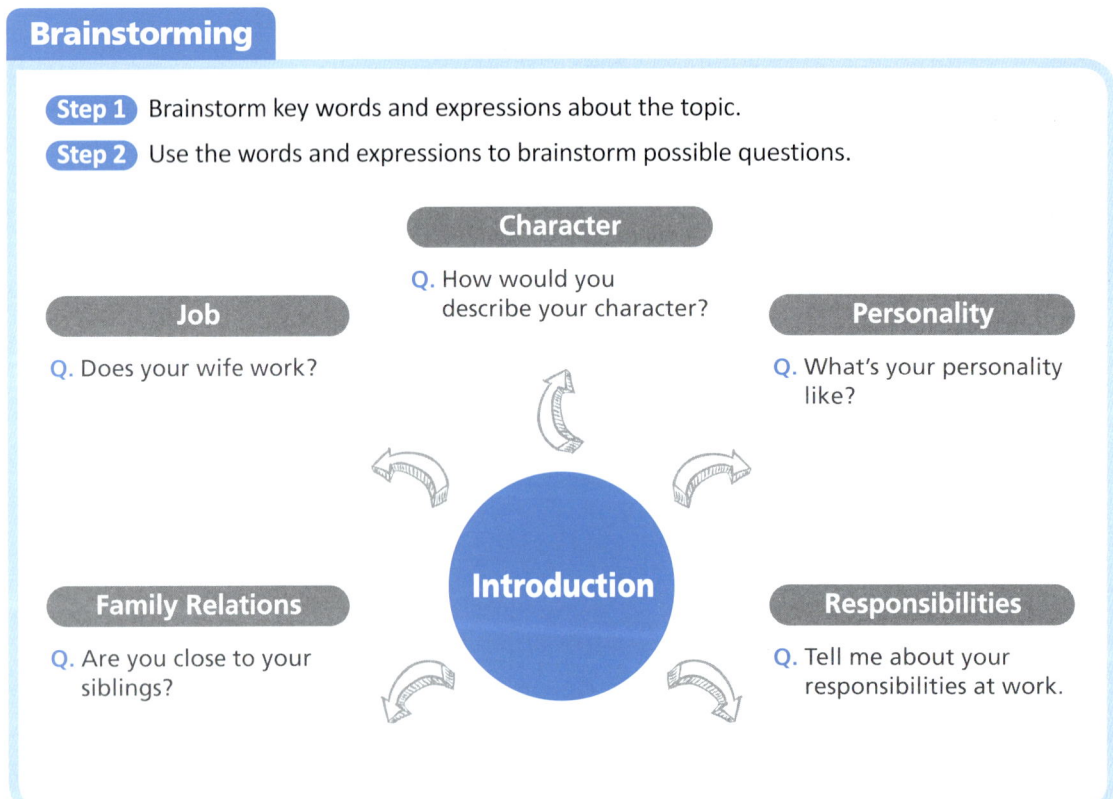

Skill up! Expressions

Useful Expressions

이름과 나이
Hello. My name is David, and I am **36 years old**.
안녕하세요, 제 이름은 데이빗이고 36살입니다.

나이
in my late 20's
in my mid 30's
in my early 40's

가족관계 및 결혼여부
I have **a younger brother and an older sister**.
저에게는 남동생 하나, 누나 하나가 있습니다.

I am **married with two children**.
저는 결혼을 했고 2명의 자녀가 있습니다.

가족관계 및 결혼여부
be an only child
have two siblings
live at home with my parents
live alone
be married with a young son[no children]

직업
I **work for** a company called ABC.
저는 ABC라는 회사에서 일합니다.

직업
work at a bank
work as a marketing supervisor

성격 및 취미
I am always at the **center of attention**.
저는 항상 주목의 대상입니다.

I love to **hang out with friends**.
저는 친구들과 어울리는 것을 좋아합니다.

I am happiest **spending time alone**.
전 혼자 시간을 보낼 때 가장 행복합니다.

I consider myself to be **sociable** because I love to talk to people.
전 대화하는 것을 좋아하기 때문에 스스로를 사교적이라고 생각합니다.

성격 및 취미
decision maker
one who plans everything
person people ask for advice
go out with a group

read on weekends
watch TV
play computer games

adventurous l ambitious l
confident l energetic l
enthusiastic l funny l faithful l
friendly l humorous l joyful l
open-minded l outgoing l
optimistic l passionate l

외모
People think I am **pretty**, but I think I am **very plain looking**.
남들은 저보고 예쁘다고 하는데 전 굉장히 평범한 얼굴이라고 생각합니다.

외모
tall and thin
short and a bit overweight

How to Answer

Q1. Let's start the interview now. Please tell me a little about yourself.

내용구성하기					
	Introduction	☑ 이름과 나이			
	Body	☑ 현재 하는 일	☑ 나의 성격	☑ 가족관계 및 사는 곳	☑ 취미
	Closing	☑ 느낌 및 의견			

Introduction

이름&나이 My name is Suhyeon Kim, but I also go by James. I am in my late 30's. I would like to tell you a little more about myself.

Body

현재 하는 일 I have been a marketing manager at Doosan for 10 years.

나의 성격 My co-workers say I am a humorous, ambitious, and a sociable person, but my family and friends see me as a warm and caring person.

가족관계 I've been married for six years. There are 4 people in my family, my hard-working and attractive wife, a naughty but funny son, a shy daughter, and me.

사는 곳 I live in the Gangnam district of Seoul. It's very close to where I work.

취미 In my free time, I go bike riding with my family.

Closing

느낌 및 의견 I have a busy life full of fun and joy.

제 이름은 김수현이고, 제임스라고도 부릅니다. 나이는 30대입니다. 저에 대해 조금 더 소개해드리겠습니다. 저는 두산에서 10년간 마케팅 매니저로 일하고 있습니다. 동료들은 제가 유머러스하며 포부가 있고 사교적인 사람이라고 말하지만 제 가족, 친구들은 저를 온화하고 세심한 사람이라고 합니다. 결혼한지 6년 됐고 제 가족은 성실하고 매력적인 아내와 장난꾸러기인 아들, 수줍은 성격의 딸 그리고 저까지 총 4명입니다. 저는 서울 강남구에 살고 있는데 직장과 매우 가깝습니다. 여가시간에는 가족과 자전거를 타러 갑니다. 즐거움으로 가득한 바쁜 생활을 보내고 있습니다.

답변 tip!

첫인상을 결정하는 질문인 만큼 자기소개를 충분히 연습해두는 것이 중요합니다. 자기소개를 가장 자연스럽게 풀어가는 방법은 이름과 나이, 하는 일, 가족관계, 성격, 취미 및 여가활동 등에 관하여 이야기하면 됩니다. 성격 및 외모에 관한 형용사들을 충분히 활용하여 답변내용을 풍부히 구성하는 것이 중요합니다.

Q2. Please tell me briefly about yourself and your family.

내용구성하기	Introduction	☑ 이름과 나이			
	Body	☑ 현재 하는 일	☑ 가족관계 및 사는 곳	☑ 나의 성격	☑ 취미
	Closing	☑ 느낌 및 의견			

Introduction

이름&나이 My name is Soomin Kim. I am in my 30's. I will tell you a bit more about myself.

Body

현재 하는 일 I work for a company called Samsung Electronics as an engineer. I've worked at this company for 10 years.

가족관계 및 사는 곳 I live in Suwon with my wife, son, and daughter. It's close to my office. I often go to a park near my house with my family on the weekends.

나의 성격 In terms of my personality, my friends say I am active and positive.

취미 As for my interests, I like cooking. I sometimes cook for my family. Feeding them delicious food makes me happy.

Closing

느낌 및 의견 I live a busy life but I'm happy with the people around me.

제 이름은 김수민이고 나이는 30대입니다. 제 소개를 조금 더 하겠습니다. 저는 삼성전자에서 엔지니어로 일하고 있습니다. 이 회사에선 10년 동안 근무하고 있습니다. 아내, 아들, 딸과 수원에서 살고 있는데 집은 사무실과 가까운 위치에 있습니다. 주말에는 가족과 집 근처 공원에 자주 갑니다. 제 성격에 대해 말해보자면 친구들은 저를 활동적이고 긍정적이라고 얘기합니다. 제 취미는 요리입니다. 가끔 가족을 위해 요리를 합니다. 맛있는 음식을 먹는 가족을 보면 행복해지죠. 바쁜 생활이지만 제 주변 사람들과 행복하게 지내고 있습니다.

고득점 tip!

'자기소개하기', '성격과 자기소개하기', '가족과 자기소개하기' 등 자기소개에 중요시하는 부분을 포함한 다양한 질문이 나옵니다. 질문을 잘 듣고 추가질문에 대한 내용을 빠뜨리지 않고 답변하도록 합니다. Eva에게 말하는 것 같은 친근한 표현을 대답 앞뒤에 사용하는 것도 좋습니다.

My Answer — Use the expressions in the Skill Up section to develop your sentences.

- Introduction

- Body

- Closing

OPIc
도전! IM+

UNIT 2

인물 묘사

UNIT 02 인물 묘사

OPIc 도전! IM+

Learning Objectives

본인주위의 인물이나 특정 직업의 인물을 묘사할 수 있다.

Frequently Asked Questions

- Please tell me about your family.
- Tell me something about yourself and your best friend.
- Would you please tell me about one of your closest neighbors?
- Can you tell me about a co-worker?
- You said you live with your family. Please tell me more about your family. What activities do you do with your family?

Brainstorming

Step 1 Brainstorm key words and expressions about the topic.
Step 2 Use the words and expressions to brainstorm possible questions.

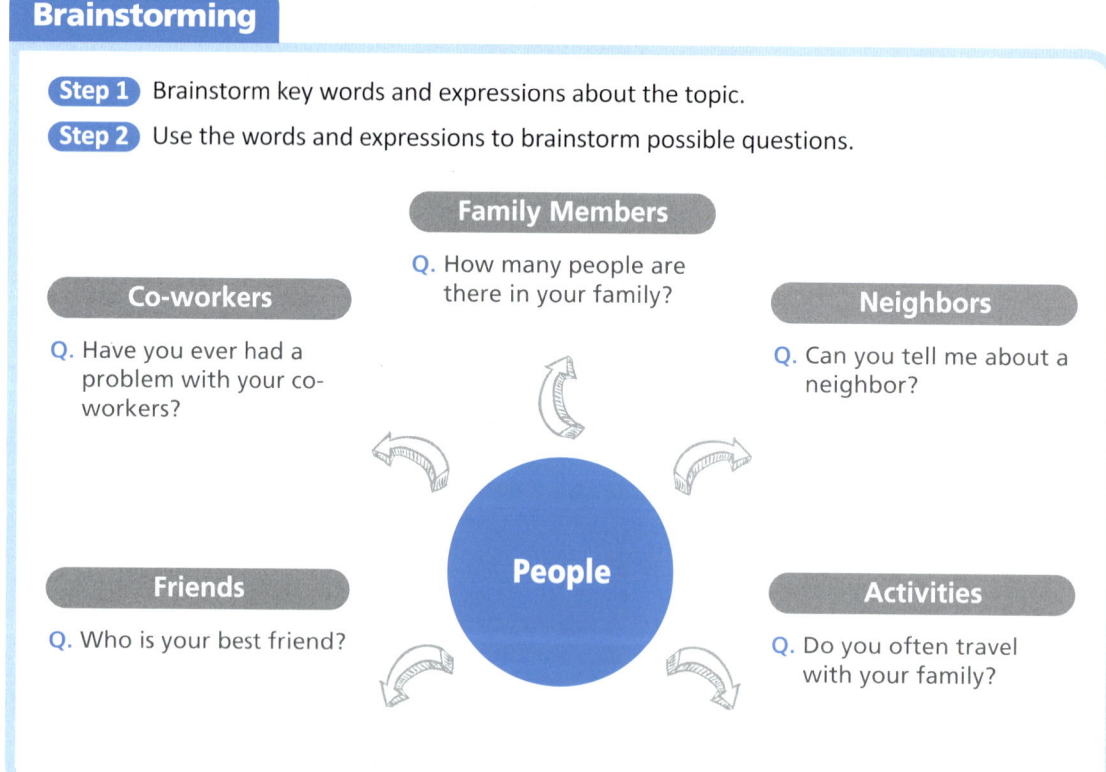

Family Members
Q. How many people are there in your family?

Co-workers
Q. Have you ever had a problem with your co-workers?

Neighbors
Q. Can you tell me about a neighbor?

Friends
Q. Who is your best friend?

Activities
Q. Do you often travel with your family?

People

Skill up! Expressions

Useful Expressions

가족, 친구 소개

There are four people in my family: my wife, two sons, and me.
가족은 아내, 아들 두 명 그리고 저까지 4명입니다.

I am married and have two children.
결혼해서 자녀 2명을 두고 있습니다.

I would like to tell you about my sister; Jenna and I are best friends.
제 여동생인 제나와 저는 가장 친한 친구입니다.

I've known my best friend **since high school**.
고등학교 때부터 친한 친구가 있습니다.

가족 / 친구 소개
Let me tell you about...

알고 지내온 기간
have been friends for + 기간
have know each other for + 기간
since my college days
since I lived in America

성격묘사

My brother is **very independent and sociable**.
제 남동생은 아주 독립적이고 사교적입니다.

상대방 성격묘사
shy and quiet
kind and considerate
thoughtful but self-centered
humorous and ambitious

일상생활 및 직업

My girlfriend is a thin, beautiful woman who **works at a coffee shop** near my apartment.
제 여자친구는 아주 날씬하고 아름답습니다. 제가 사는 아파트 근처 커피숍에서 일하고 있습니다.

My wife is a full-time housewife.
제 아내는 전업 주부입니다.

일상생활 및 직업
work for a bank
be a colleague in my office

함께 하는 활동

My friends and I always **have a good time together**.
친구들과 함께 늘 즐거운 시간을 보냅니다.

We **usually** go to the movies together **once a month**.
우리는 보통 한 달에 한번 영화를 보러 갑니다.

I enjoy traveling with family once or twice a year.
가족과 일 년에 한두 번 여행을 갑니다.

함께 하는 활동
watch sports at a bar
go drinking on Fridays
play soccer
at the park
spend lots of time
like to go clubbing

when I feel down
when I'm bored
when I have free time

How to Answer

Q1. Please tell me about your family.

내용구성하기	Introduction	☑ 가족 구성원 소개			
	Body	☑ 외모	☑ 성격	☑ 취미	☑ 함께하는 활동
	Closing	☑ 느낌 및 의견			

Introduction

가족 구성원 소개 I will tell you about my family. There are four people in my family: two daughters, my wife, and me.

Body

외모, 성격&취미 My first daughter is 12 years old. She has big eyes and long hair. She likes her long hair. She is very active. My second daughter is 9 years old. She has a beautiful face and she is slim. She likes drawing. Lastly, my wife is two years younger than me. She has big eyes and a round face. She runs a small accessory shop. She makes accessories and teaches others how to make them there.

함께 하는 활동 We do many things together on the weekend like traveling, watching movies, and cooking.

Closing

느낌 및 의견 I think I have a beautiful family.

가족 소개를 하겠습니다. 우리 가족은 딸 두 명, 아내, 그리고 저 이렇게 총 넷입니다. 큰 딸은 12살입니다. 큰 눈에 쌍꺼풀이 있고 머리가 긴데 본인의 긴 머리를 좋아합니다. 활동적인 아이입니다. 둘째 딸은 9살입니다. 둘째도 쌍꺼풀이 있는 큰 눈에 얼굴이 예쁘고 마른 몸매입니다. 그림 그리는 것을 좋아합니다. 마지막으로 제 아내는 저보다 2살 아래로 눈이 크고 얼굴이 동그란 편입니다. 작은 액세서리 가게를 운영하고 있습니다. 직접 액세서리를 만들고 만드는 방법을 다른 사람들에게 가르쳐줍니다. 주말에는 가족끼리 여행을 가거나, 영화를 보거나, 요리를 하는 등 다양한 활동을 함께 합니다. 아름다운 가족이라고 생각합니다.

답변 tip!

자기자신 외에 직장동료, 친구 혹은 이웃을 소개하라는 질문이 흔히 등장합니다. 소개하는 대상과의 친분 정보 및 알고 지내온 기간, 외모, 성격,일상생활 및 생활 태도, 나와 함께 하는 활동 등을 서술해주면 좋습니다. 마지막으로 상대방에 대한 나의 느낌 및 의견을 언급해주면 훌륭한 답변이 될 수 있습니다.

Q2. Tell me something about your best friend.

내용구성하기	Introduction	☑ 친구 소개				
	Body	☑ 알고 지낸 기간	☑ 성격	☑ 외모	☑ 특징	☑ 함께 하는 활동
	Closing	☑ 느낌 및 의견				

Introduction

친구 소개 I would like to tell you about my best friend, Bill. We have known each other for more than 15 years.

Body

알고 지낸 기간 Currently, we work in the Marketing Department of Samsung together.

성격 I think Bill is a generous person. He often buys coffee for our department.

외모 As for his appearance, Bill is a neat and clean person. He is quite tall and very muscular. He also has short hair and wears glasses.

특징 When it comes to work, he always shows up for meetings on time, and he often says useful things.

함께 하는 활동 About twice a week, we go for a drink together after work.

Closing

느낌 및 의견 Everyone loves working with Bill, and I also like him very much.

제 가장 친한 친구인 빌에 대한 얘기해보겠습니다. 우린 15년 동안 알고 지낸 사이입니다. 현재 삼성의 마케팅 부서에서 함께 일하고 있죠. 빌은 관대합니다. 종종 부서 전체에 커피를 사주기도 합니다. 외모에 대해 설명해 보겠습니다. 빌은 깔끔하고 말쑥합니다. 키가 크고 근육질입니다. 짧은 머리에 안경을 쓰고 있습니다. 일 문제에 있어선 항상 제시간에 회의에 와서 유용한 제안을 합니다. 일주일에 두 번 정도는 퇴근 후 함께 술을 마시러 갑니다. 다들 빌과 일하는 것을 좋아합니다. 저 역시 그를 참 좋아합니다.

고득점 tip!

여러명을 소개할 때에는 Body에서 한명씩 순차적으로 설명하고, 한명에 대해 소개할 때에는 그사람에 대한 성격, 외모, 함께하는 활동등을 차례대로 설명합니다. 외모를 묘사할 때 'fat', 'ugly'와 같은 부정적인 표현은 피하는 것이 좋습니다.

Use the expressions in the Skill Up section to develop your sentences.

— Introduction

— Body

— Closing

OPIc 도전! IM+

UNIT 3

장소 묘사

UNIT 03 장소 묘사

OPIc 도전! IM+

Learning Objectives

장소의 위치, 역할 및 기능, 특징 등에 대해 묘사하거나, 특정 장소와 개인 혹은 조직의 관계, 그리고 장소에 대한 개인적인 생각과 의견에 대해 답할 수 있다.

Frequently Asked Questions

- Please tell me about where you live. Do you live in an apartment or a house? What does it look like? How many rooms does it have?
- Please tell me about your house. What's your favorite room? Why do you like that room?
- Can you think of any memorable events that happened in your house?
- I would like to know about your neighborhood.

Brainstorming

Step 1 Brainstorm key words and expressions about the topic.
Step 2 Use the words and expressions to brainstorm possible questions.

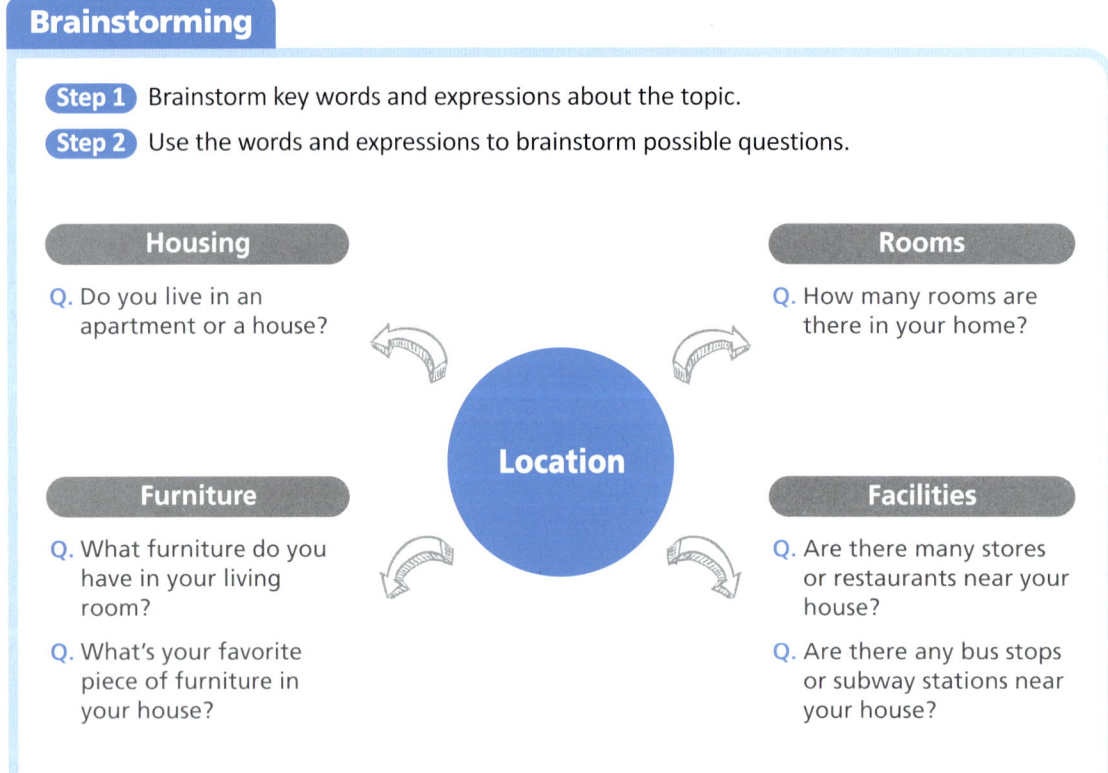

Housing
Q. Do you live in an apartment or a house?

Rooms
Q. How many rooms are there in your home?

Location

Furniture
Q. What furniture do you have in your living room?
Q. What's your favorite piece of furniture in your house?

Facilities
Q. Are there many stores or restaurants near your house?
Q. Are there any bus stops or subway stations near your house?

Skill up! Expressions

집의 위치, 주거 형태

I live in Suwon, which is near Seoul.
저는 서울 근처에 있는 수원에 살고 있습니다.

I live in **an apartment**.
저는 주택/원룸/아파트/기숙사에 살고 있습니다.

The place where I live is a **small apartment** in a residential area.
제가 사는 곳은 주거 지역의 소형 아파트입니다.

I live on the 10th floor of a 12-story apartment building.
저는 12층짜리 아파트의 10층에 살고 있습니다.

집의 구조 및 가구

My house has **three bedrooms, one living room, and a kitchen**.
우리 집에는 방 3개, 거실과 주방이 있습니다.

When you come into my house, you will see the living room first.
집에 들어오면 제일 먼저 거실이 보입니다.

There is a master bedroom next to the living room.
거실 옆에 안방이 있습니다.

There is **a desk, a bed, a bedside table, and a bookcase** in my room.
제 방에는 책상, 침대, 협탁과 책장이 있습니다.

집의 분위기 및 장점

The view from my apartment is really beautiful at night.
아파트에서 보이는 야경은 정말 아름답습니다.

My room is neat (well-organized, messy, cozy).
제 방은 깔끔합니다 (잘 정리되어 있습니다, 지저분합니다, 아늑합니다).

It is a nice place to live.
살기 좋은 곳입니다.

Useful Expressions

집의 위치, 주거형태
house | studio | dormitory

medium sized house
large apartment
spacious apartment

집구조 및 가구
bathroom
dressing room
baby's room
guest room
dining room
uility room
balcony
dressing table
book shelf
a coffee table
a dining table
a couch

집분위기 및 장정
comfortable
sweet
lovely
well-organized
messy
cozy
convenient

How to Answer

Q1. Please tell me about where you live. Do you live in an apartment or a house? What does it look like? How many rooms does it have?

내용구성하기		
	Introduction	☑ 집의 위치, 형태
	Body	☑ 집의 구조 ☑ 가구 ☑ 하는 활동 ☑ 집 주변 환경
	Closing	☑ 느낌 및 의견

Introduction

집의 위치 및 형태 I will tell you about my house. I live in a 3-story apartment building. I live on the first floor; there are two bedrooms, one living room, and one bathroom.

Body

집의 구조 및 가구 From the outside, the building doesn't look fancy or new but I like the interior of my house. When you come into my home, you will see the spacious entryway first. There are five bookshelves along the wall. I like reading books, so I have many books. If you go inside a bit further, you can see the spacious living room. There is a sofa, a big TV, and a table there.

하는 활동 On the weekend, my wife plays the piano while I read books in the living room.

집 주변 환경 Moreover, near my house, there are various amenities such as a supermarket, a pharmacy, a bakery, and a dry cleaner's.

Closing

느낌 및 의견 My house is not really that special but it is the perfect place for my wife and I to live.

우리 집에 대해 얘기하겠습니다. 저는 3층짜리 아파트에 살고 있습니다. 전 1층에 삽니다. 침실 2개, 거실, 화장실이 있습니다. 밖에서 보면 화려해 보이는 건물은 아니지만 집의 인테리어가 맘에 듭니다. 집에 들어오면 널찍한 현관이 눈에 띕니다. 벽에는 5개의 책 선반이 붙어 있습니다. 저는 독서를 좋아해서 책이 많습니다. 집안으로 좀더 들어오면 역시 넓은 거실이 눈에 들어옵니다. 소파와 대형 TV, 테이블이 놓여 있습니다. 주말에는 거실에서 아내는 피아노를 치고 전 책을 읽습니다. 게다가 집 근처에 슈퍼마켓, 약국, 빵집, 세탁소 같은 다양한 편의시설이 있습니다. 그렇게 특별한 집은 아니지만 아내와 제가 살기에는 완벽한 곳입니다.

답변 tip!

장소묘사와 관련된 문제 유형으로 자신이 살고 있는 집이나 동네와 관련된 문제들이 자주 등장 합니다. 우리 집의 구조가 어떻게 되는지, 집 주변에는 무엇이 있는지를 미리 관찰하고 답변을 정리해 두면 좋습니다.

Q2. I would like to know about your neighborhood.

내용구성하기
- **Introduction** ☑ 동네 소개
- **Body** ☑ 동네를 좋아하는 이유 3가지
- **Closing** ☑ 느낌 및 의견

Introduction
동네 소개 I will tell you about my neighborhood, I like it for several reasons.

Body
좋아하는 이유 ① 지리적 위치 First of all, my company is located near my home. It takes just 10 minutes to get there by car. That's the main reason why I chose this house. I don't have to waste time commuting.

좋아하는 이유 ② 편의시설 Secondly, there are many stores near my house, such as a supermarket, a dry cleaner's, and restaurants. It is within walking distance to the shops, so it takes just ten minutes to get there on foot.

좋아하는 이유 ③ 주변 환경 Lastly, the atmosphere is so peaceful. It is the best place to relax after work.

Closing
느낌 및 의견 Those are the reasons why I like my neighborhood.

동네 얘기를 해보겠습니다. 이곳을 좋아하는 이유가 몇 가지 있습니다. 먼저 집에서 회사가 가깝습니다. 자동차로 10분 정도 걸립니다. 이 집을 고른 건 그 이유가 가장 큽니다. 출퇴근에 시간을 허비하고 싶지 않아서요. 상점들은 모두 걸어서 갈 수 있는 거리에 위치해 있는데 도보로 10분 밖에 걸리지 않습니다. 마지막으로 굉장히 평화로운 분위기입니다. 일을 마친 후 휴식하기에 최적의 장소죠. 이런 점들이 제가 우리 동네를 좋아하는 이유입니다.

고득점 tip!

주제에 맞는 키워드를 3가지 생각하고 말하기를 시작하면 쉽습니다. 집을 묘사할 때 집안에서 보이는 것들만 묘사하기보다는 집 주변에 있는 시설이나 주위 환경을 함께 묘사하면 좋습니다.

My Answer — Use the expressions in the Skill Up section to develop your sentences.

- Introduction

- Body

- Closing

실력다지기

☑ Part 2 설문주제

Unit 4	직장생활
Unit 5	영화보기
Unit 6	카페가기
Unit 7	바/펍 가기
Unit 8	공원가기
Unit 9	해변가기
Unit 10	음악 감상하기
Unit 11	조깅/걷기
Unit 12	국내 여행
Unit 13	해외 여행
Unit 14	집에서 보내는 휴가

OPIc
도전!
IM+

OPIc
도전! IM+

UNIT 4

직장생활

UNIT 04 직장생활

OPIc 도전 IM+

Learning Objectives

회사의 역사 및 규모, 업무관련 등 회사 전반 사항에 관련된 질문에 답할 수 있다.

Frequently Asked Questions

- Can you tell me about the company you work for? What kind of business is it? Please describe your company in as much detail as possible.
- What is your job title, and what kind of work do you do? Tell me about your responsibilities.
- Please tell me about your typical day at work. What do you usually do as soon as you arrive at the office?
- Can you tell me about your lunch time at work? Where do you usually have lunch? Who do you have lunch with?

Brainstorming

Step 1 Brainstorm key words and expressions about the topic.
Step 2 Use the words and expressions to brainstorm possible questions.

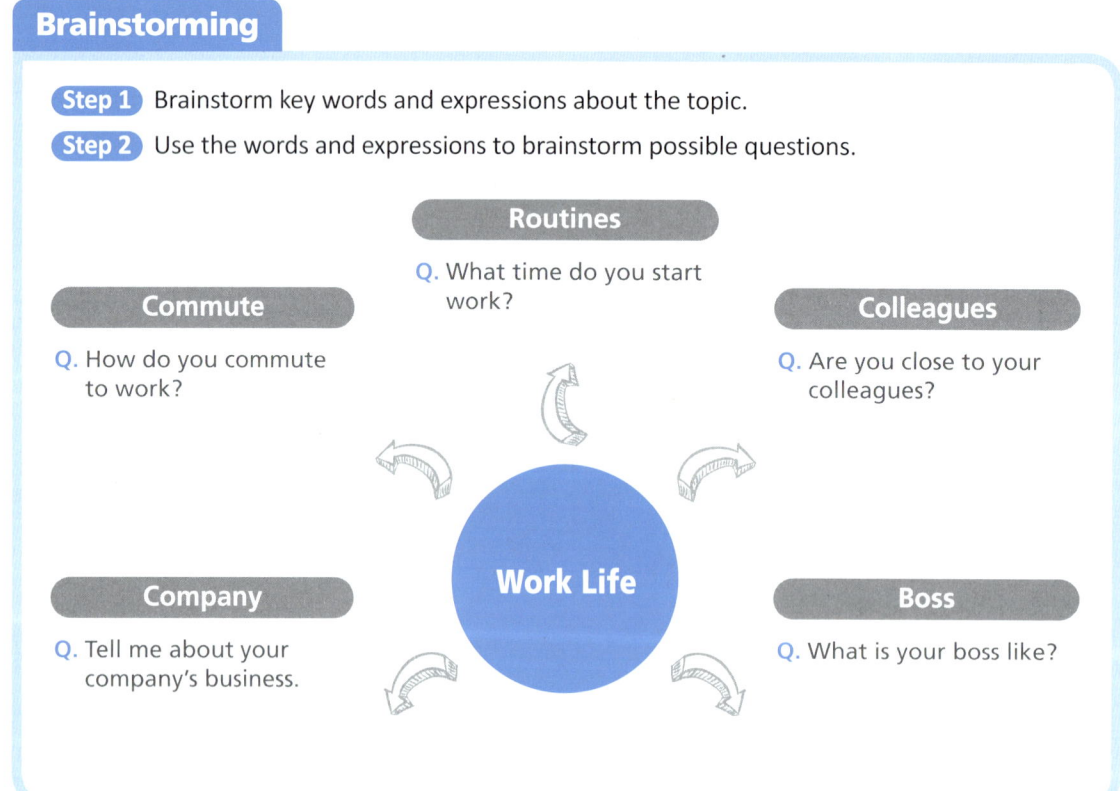

Routines
Q. What time do you start work?

Commute
Q. How do you commute to work?

Colleagues
Q. Are you close to your colleagues?

Company
Q. Tell me about your company's business.

Boss
Q. What is your boss like?

Work Life

Skill up! Expressions

직장명, 근무지

I work at an electronics company, which sells cell phones.
저는 휴대폰을 판매하는 전자 회사에서 근무하고 있습니다.

The company is located in the center of Seoul.
회사는 서울 중심부에 위치해 있습니다.

회사 관련 추가 설명

It is the one of the **biggest companies** in Korea.
한국에서 가장 큰 대기업 중 하나입니다.

My company **manufactures** electrical components for the computer industry.
컴퓨터 산업용 전자 부품들을 제조하는 회사입니다.

The company was **founded over** 20 years ago.
회사는 설립된 지 20년이 넘었습니다.

담당 업무 및 일과

I am a salesman **responsible for** software sales.
전 영업사원으로 소프트웨어 영업을 맡고 있습니다.

I go to the office at around 8:30 a.m.
전 사무실에 8시 30분쯤 도착합니다.

I attend a business meeting for about an hour in the morning.
오전에 한 시간 정도 비즈니스 회의에 참석합니다.

I have lunch at 12 with my co-workers at the company cafeteria.
12시에 동료들과 회사 식당에서 점심을 먹습니다.

느낌 및 의견

I'm satisfied with what I do and the people I work with.
제가 하고 있는 일과 동료들에게 모두 만족합니다.

Useful Expressions

근무지
work for

연혁
be established [found] in 년도

규모
major[large] company
small and medium-sized company

생산품
produce | develop | provide

담당업무
deal with
handle
in charge of

하루 업무일과
check e-mails
copy documents
evaluate products
report on progress
go over reports
keep a daily work log
review project specifications
submit a proposal

퇴근 및 야근
get off work
work by night

출퇴근 시간을 보내는 방법
read a free newspaper
watch the game
watch the scenery
watch a movie
pass the time reading a book

출퇴근 교통 체증
get caught up in
frequently get slowed down in

출퇴근길 묘사
be crowded
be full of cars
be at a standstill
caught [stuck up] in a traffic jam

How to Answer

Q1. Can you tell me about the company you work for? What kind of business is it? Please describe your company in as much detail as possible.

내용구성하기					
	Introduction	☑ 회사이름 및 사업분야			
	Body	☑ 회사 설립 연도	☑ 회사 위치	☑ 주요 사업	☑ 주력 상품
	Closing	☑ 느낌 및 의견			

Introduction

회사이름 및 사업분야 I work for a large software development company named Excel Corporation.

Body

회사 설립 연도 Excel was founded over 10 years ago.

회사 위치 The company's offices are located in Seoul and Incheon.

주요 사업 The company develops office system software for large multi-national companies.

주력 상품 The software package is an integrated system that can handle all aspects of a company's day-to-day business. The unique thing about the software is that it is designed to be an easy-to-use business solution.

Closing

느낌 및 의견 The future of my company looks bright and working for Excel is very interesting.

저는 엑셀 코퍼레이션이란 대형 소프트웨어 개발 회사에서 일하고 있습니다. 엑셀 사는 설립된 지 10년이 넘었습니다. 회사 사무실은 서울과 인천에 있습니다. 우리 회사는 다국적 기업들을 위한 사무용 소프트웨어를 개발하고 있습니다. 이 소프트웨어 패키지는 기업의 일상 업무를 전반적으로 모두 처리할 수 있는 통합 시스템입니다. 이 소프트웨어의 특징은 사용하기 쉬운 비즈니스 솔루션용으로 설계됐다는 점입니다. 회사 전망이 밝아서 엑셀사에서 일하는 게 재미있습니다.

답변 tip!

회사와 업무관련에 대한 질문이 연달아 출제될 가능성이 높습니다. 회사의 역사 및 규모 등 회사 전반 사항에 관한 질문들을 미리 준비해두는 것이 좋습니다. 또한 자신의 업무 및 프로젝트에 관하여 답변을 정리해 보도록 합니다.

Q2. Please tell me about your typical day at work. What do you usually do as soon as you arrive at the office?

내용구성하기	Introduction	☑ 회사 생활		
	Body	☑ 오전에 하는 일	☑ 점심시간	☑ 오후에 하는 일
	Closing	☑ 느낌 및 의견		

Introduction
회사 생활 I will tell you about my typical day at work.

Body
오전에 하는 일 I get to the office around 8 a.m. I usually have a meeting with my co-workers in the morning. After the meeting, I work on my project.

점심시간 I have lunch with my co-workers at the company cafeteria at 12. They serve 7 or 8 different kinds of food every day. My favorite thing to eat there is Korean food like kimchi stew.

오후에 하는 일 After lunch, I am busier in the afternoon and have to attend a lot of meetings. That's why I usually stay late at the office until 8 or 9 p.m.

Closing
느낌 및 의견 Even though I am very busy, I really enjoy my work.

직장에서의 하루 일과에 대해 얘기해보겠습니다. 저는 8시 정도에 사무실에 도착해서 동료들과 오전 회의를 가집니다. 회의 후에는 제 프로젝트 업무를 진행합니다. 12시에 회사 식당에서 동료들과 점심을 먹습니다. 회사 식당은 매일 다양한 7-8가지 종류의 음식을 제공합니다. 제가 제일 좋아하는 음식은 김치나 찌개 같은 한식입니다. 점심식사 후 오후에는 조금 더 바쁘며 여러 회의에 참석해야 합니다. 그래서 보통 8시나 9시의 늦은 시간까지 사무실에 남게 됩니다. 매우 바쁘지만 전 제 일을 즐깁니다.

고득점 tip!

직장인들의 하루 일과와 관련하여 출퇴근에 대한 질문이 출제될 가능성이 높습니다. 출퇴근 시 교통수단과 소요 시간, 출퇴근 시간을 보내는 방법, 출퇴근길 묘사, 출근 전후의 일과, 출퇴근 시 겪었던 에피소드 등에 관한 질문들이 주어집니다. 이에 관하여 자신만의 답안을 정리해 두는 것이 좋습니다.

 **My Answer** Use the expressions in the Skill Up section to develop your sentences.

− Introduction

− Body

− Closing

OPIc
도전! IM+

UNIT 5
영화보기

UNIT 05 영화보기

OPIc 도전! IM+

Learning Objectives

좋아하는 영화의 내용, 배우, 기억에 남는 영화 등에 관해 말할 수 있다.

Frequently Asked Questions

- How often do you watch movies? Do you ever go to the movies alone? Who do you like to go with?
- What kind of movie do you enjoy watching? Why do you like watching those kinds of movies?
- Tell me about the movie theater you go to most often. Where is it? Why do you prefer that theater?
- Please tell me about the most memorable movie you have ever watched. What was the movie about? Who was in it?

Brainstorming

Step 1 Brainstorm key words and expressions about the topic.
Step 2 Use the words and expressions to brainstorm possible questions.

Movie Stars
Q. Who is your favorite actor?
Q. Why do you like them?

Favorite Movies
Q. What kind of movie do you like?
Q. What's your favorite movie?

Movie Theaters
Q. Which movie theater do you go to most often?

Movies

Skill up! Expressions

Useful Expressions

좋아하는 영화, 영화 장르

I like all kinds of movies except horror movies.
공포 영화를 제외한 모든 장르의 영화를 좋아합니다.

My favorite movies are action and **romantic movies**.
제일 좋아하는 건 액션과 로맨틱 영화입니다.

I really like watching **romantic comedies**.
로맨틱 코미디 영화도 정말 좋아합니다.

I like these kinds of movies because they are **educational**.
이런 종류의 영화를 좋아하는 이유는 교육적이기 때문입니다.

Action movies always make me feel **excited**.
액션 영화는 항상 신납니다.

Those movies are **fun** and **entertaining**.
이러한 영화는 재미와 즐거움을 줍니다.

좋아하는 장르
horror | thriller |
martial arts |
independent films |
science fiction | adventure

영화 보는 패턴

On weekends, I go to the theater.
주말에는 영화관에 갑니다.

I often go to the movies with my husband on the weekend.
주말에는 남편과 영화관에 자주 갑니다.

I prefer going to the movies early in the afternoon on Sunday.
일요일 이른 오후에 영화 보러 가는 것을 좋아합니다.

I usually choose a movie **after checking the movie listings**.
영화 목록을 확인한 후에 영화를 선택합니다.

관람 전후 활동
read reviews
see what's showing
check the available seats
book a ticket
buy tickets
at the theater box office
grab a bite
write movie reviews on a blog

극장

The movie theater I usually go to is a brand new multiplex theater near my house.
제가 주로 가는 영화관은 집근처에 새로 생긴 멀티플렉스 영화관입니다.

The movie theater has many screens and comfortable seats.
그 영화관은 상영관이 많고 좌석도 편안합니다.

I can get a discount with my membership card.
멤버십 카드로 할인을 받을 수 있습니다.

감상
touching | moving | joyful |
melancholy | satisfying |
sympathetic | uplifting |
stimulating | refreshing |
encouraging | motivating |
peaceful

www.carrotenglish.com

How to Answer

Q1. Tell me about the movie theater you go to most often. Where is it? Why do you prefer that theater?

내용구성하기		
	Introduction	☑ 극장 이름 및 위치
	Body	☑ 극장에 가는 이유 3가지
	Closing	☑ 느낌 및 의견

Introduction

자주 가는 영화관 이름 및 위치 I'll tell you about my favorite movie theater. My favorite movie theater is the CGV located in Pyeongchon. There are a few reasons why I prefer it to other theaters.

Body

극장에 가는 이유 ① 지리적 위치 First of all, it's close to my house. It takes me about 10 minutes by foot.

극장에 가는 이유 ② 시설 Also, it has many screens, so I have many choices. They even have 3D, 4D, and IMAX theaters there.

극장에 가는 이유 ② 주변편의시설 Lastly, the theater is brand new with many convenient facilities. It has comfortable seats with a lot of leg room. There are many cafes, restaurants, and stores around, so I can do many other activities before and after watching a movie.

Closing

느낌 및 의견 For these reasons, I prefer this movie theater.

제일 좋아하는 영화관에 대해 이야기해보겠습니다. 제가 가장 좋아하는 영화관은 평촌에 있는 CGV입니다. 다른 영화관보다 이곳을 더 좋아하는 몇 가지 이유가 있습니다. 먼저 집에서 가깝습니다. 도보로 10분밖에 걸리지 않죠. 또한 상영관이 많아서 선택의 폭이 넓습니다. 3D, 4D에 아이맥스 상영관까지 갖추고 있죠. 마지막으로 이 극장은 여러 편의시설이 겸비된 신형 극장입니다. 좌석도 편안하고 다리를 뻗을 수 있는 공간이 넓습니다. 카페, 레스토랑, 상점들도 많아서 영화를 보기 전후로 다양한 활동을 즐길 수 있습니다. 이러한 이유로 전 이 영화관을 선호합니다.

답변 tip!

영화보기는 여가활동 주제 중 많이 선호하는 항목입니다. 이와 관련하여 출제되는 대표적인 문항유형들은 1) 관람패턴(누구와 언제, 얼마나 자주 관람하는지), 2) 좋아하는 장르, 3) 자주 가는 장소 묘사, 4) 특별한 경험 및 관람 전후 활동 등에 대한 것입니다. 해당 문항유형에 대한 표현들을 익혀 자세하게 설명하는 연습을 하도록 합니다.

Q2. Please tell me about the most memorable movie you have watched. What was the movie about? Who was in it?

내용구성하기	Introduction	☑ 최신 본 영화 이름		
	Body	☑ 영화 배우	☑ 영화 내용	☑ 영화를 본 후의 느낌
	Closing	☑ 느낌 및 의견		

Introduction
최신 본 영화 이름 I like watching movies of all genres. Recently, I saw a movie called Sully.

Body
영화 배우 및 영화 내용 Tom Hanks starred in it. The movie is about an American pilot. He became a hero after landing his damaged plane on the Hudson River. He saves the flight's passengers and crew.

영화를 본 후의 느낌 It is a fun and entertaining movie. Also, it is very touching.

Closing
느낌 및 의견 I think Sully is the best movie of this year. If you haven't seen it yet, you must watch it.

전 모든 장르의 영화를 즐겨 봅니다. 최근에는 설리라는 영화를 봤습니다. 톰 행크스가 출연한 영화로 미국인 비행사에 관한 영화였습니다. 그는 허드슨 강에 고장 난 비행기로 착륙해 영웅이 되었습니다. 비행기 승객과 승무원의 목숨을 구한 것이죠. 재미있는 영화였습니다. 또한 매우 감동적이기도 했습니다. 제 생각에 설리는 올해 최고의 영화입니다. 아직 못 보셨다면 꼭 보세요.

고득점 tip!
영화 보기와 TV 시청하기의 문제들은 비슷할 뿐만 아니라 답변의 내용에서 유사점들이 많아 함께 학습하면 효율적으로 준비할 수 있습니다. 좋아하는 영화 장르나 좋아하는 영화 배우 등의 문제가 나올 수 있으니 질문을 잘 듣고 알맞은 답변을 하도록 합니다.

Use the expressions in the Skill Up section to develop your sentences.

- Introduction

- Body

- Closing

OPIc 도전! IM+

UNIT 6

카페가기

UNIT 06 카페가기

OPIc 도전! IM+

Learning Objectives

자주가는 카페에 대해 묘사하고 카페에서 주로 하는 활동, 기억에 남는 경험 등을 말할 수 있다.

Frequently Asked Questions

- When do you usually go to a cafe? What do you typically order, and what do you do there?
- Tell me about your favorite cafe. Where is it located? What does it look like?
- You indicated in the survey that you enjoy drinking coffee. Please tell me about your favorite place to drink coffee. Where is it located and why do you like the place?

Brainstorming

Step 1 Brainstorm key words and expressions about the topic.
Step 2 Use the words and expressions to brainstorm possible questions.

Favorite Drink
Q. What do you usually drink at a cafe?
Q. How much is it?

Favorite Cafe
Q. What is the name of your favorite cafe?
Q. What can you see at a cafe?

Activities
Q. Do you go to a cafe alone or with someone?
Q. Do you take anything to a cafe?

Cafe

Skill up! Expressions

Useful Expressions

카페 소개

I often go to a cafe **near** my house.
저는 집 근처에 있는 카페에 자주 갑니다.

There is a cafe called Coffee in my neighborhood.
우리 동네에 있는 커피라는 카페지요.

The cafe is **small and cozy**.
작고 아늑한 카페입니다.

카페소개
close | around | by | not far from

big and luxurious
clean and simple
neat
well decorated
European style
professional

좋아하는 음료

My favorite drink to order at a cafe is black coffee.
제가 카페에서 가장 좋아하는 음료는 블랙 커피입니다.

I often go to cafes to drink a **cafe latte**.
카페에 가면 카페 라떼를 자주 마십니다.

좋아하는 음료
what I like to order
I love to drink
the drink I like the most

cappuccino | americano |
cafe mocha | green tea latte | tea |
earl grey | english breakfast |
milk tea

카페에서 하는 활동

I often **meet my friends** at a cafe.
카페에서 친구들을 종종 만납니다.

I usually **chat with my friends** at a cafe.
카페에 가면 보통 친구들과 얘기를 나눕니다.

I sometimes go to a cafe alone to **read books or study**.
때론 혼자 책을 읽거나 공부하려고 카페에 가기도 합니다.

카페에서 하는 활동
enjoy various kinds of coffee
hang out with my friends
spend time with loved ones
rearrange my thoughts

좋아하는 이유

My favorite part about the cafe is its **cozy atmosphere**.
카페에서 가장 맘에 드는 건 아늑한 분위기입니다.

It is not far from my house.
우리집 에서 그리 멀지 않습니다.

The prices there are relatively cheap.
가격도 상대적으로 저렴합니다.

좋아하는 이유
delicious drinks
lovely flatware
large parking lot
beautiful furniture
kind owner

popular among young people
owned by baristas
located near a park

it can be found easily
it has beautiful building

How to Answer

Q1. When do you usually go to a cafe? What do you typically order, and what do you do there?

내용구성하기
- **Introduction** ☑ 자주가는 카페 소개
- **Body** ☑ 카페에 가는 이유   ☑ 시설 (보이는 것)   ☑ 카페에서 하는 활동
- **Closing** ☑ 마무리

Introduction

자주가는 카페 소개 I'll tell you about what I usually do at a cafe. I often go to a coffee shop called M's Coffee near my house.

Body

카페에 가는 이유 I like to go there because it's near my house and I like its black coffee. Also, I can use the free Wi-Fi there.

카페 시설 When I walk into the cafe, there is a cashier and there are many comfortable sofas and chairs.

카페에서 하는 활동 In the cafe, I can have a chat with my family, friends, or co-workers. Sometimes, I go there alone to study or read a book.

Closing

마무리 These are the things that I normally do at a cafe.

카페에서 보통 하는 일을 말씀 드리겠습니다. 저는 집 근처에 있는 M's 커피라는 커피숍을 자주 갑니다. 그곳에 가는 이유는 집에서 가깝고 그 카페의 블랙 커피를 좋아하기 때문입니다. 또한 무료 와이파이 인터넷을 사용할 수 있습니다. 카페에 들어가면 캐셔가 있고 편안한 소파와 의자가 많습니다. 카페 안에선 가족, 친구, 동료들과 대화를 나눕니다. 공부하거나 독서를 위해 혼자 가기도 합니다. 보통 카페에 가면 그런 일을 하죠.

답변 tip!

카페가기는 2013년 뉴오픽이 도입되면서 새롭게 추가된 주제입니다. 자주 가는 카페 묘사, 카페에서 주로 하는 활동, 최근에 카페에 간 경험 등의 문제가 출제되니 예상질문에 대한 답변을 미리 준비하도록 합니다.

Q2. Tell me what you usually do at a cafe. When do you usually go? Why do you go there?

내용구성하기		
	Introduction ☑ 도입	
	Body ☑ 카페를 가는 이유	☑ 카페에서 하는 활동
	Closing ☑ 느낌 및 의견	

Introduction

도입 I enjoy drinking coffee and doing many things at cafes.

Body

카페에 가는 이유 I go to a cafe near a subway station when I have to wait for someone. There are usually many major franchises like Starbucks near stations and I can use free Wi-Fi there. Also, the tables and chairs are comfortable.

카페에서 하는 활동 ① If I go alone, I usually surf the Internet using my phone.

카페에서 하는 활동 ② But mostly, I will go to a cafe in my office building with my co-workers to hang out. I usually have a chat with them over coffee.

Closing

느낌 및 의견 Cafes are a nice place to spend time with people.

저는 카페에서 커피를 마시고 이것저것 하는 것을 좋아합니다. 누군가를 기다려야 할 일이 생기면 전철역 근처에 있는 카페에 갑니다. 전철역 근처에는 스타벅스 같은 체인점 커피숍들이 많이 있고 와이파이도 무료로 사용할 수 있는데다가 테이블과 의자도 편안합니다. 혼자 카페를 갈 경우에는 핸드폰으로 인터넷을 사용합니다. 하지만 대부분 회사 동료와 회사 건물에 위치한 카페를 가서 시간을 보냅니다. 커피를 마시면서 이야기를 나누는 편입니다. 카페는 사람과 어울리기 좋은 장소입니다.

고득점 tip!

과거에 방문했던 카페에서 있었던 경험을 말할 때에는 과거시제를 사용하는 것을 잊지 말도록 합니다. 커피 전문점을 자세하게 묘사하거나 커피의 맛을 구체적으로 설명하면 답변이 더욱 풍성해 질 수 있습니다. 'Coffee', 'cafe'를 말할 때 'F'발음에 주의 하도록 합니다.

 **My Answer** — Use the expressions in the Skill Up section to develop your sentences.

— Introduction

— Body

— Closing

OPIc
도전! IM+

UNIT 7
바/펍 가기

UNIT 07 바/펍 가기

OPIc 도전! IM+

Learning Objectives

자주가는 바/펍에 대해 묘사하고 바/펍에서 주로 하는 활동, 기억에 남는 경험 등을 말할 수 있다.

Frequently Asked Questions

- Describe the bar that you go to most often.
- When do you usually like to go to a bar? How often do you usually go there?
- Who do you go to a bar with?
- Tell me about what people normally do at bars.
- Tell me about a memorable incident you had at a bar.

Brainstorming

Step 1 Brainstorm key words and expressions about the topic.
Step 2 Use the words and expressions to brainstorm possible questions.

Drinks and Snacks
- Q. What kinds of drinks do they sell?
- Q. What's your favorite snack there?

Favorite Bar
- Q. Do you drink often?
- Q. Do you prefer bars or pubs?

Activities
- Q. Who do you usually go with?
- Q. Can you play darts or pool there?

Bar and Pub

Skill up! Expressions

바 또는 펍 소개

I often go to a pub near my office **after work**.
퇴근 후에 사무실 근처에 있는 펍에 자주 갑니다.

A bar I often go to is called Q Bar.
바라는 이름의 바에 자주 갑니다.

좋아하는 음료 및 스낵

I often drink soju with my co-workers.
동료들과 소주를 자주 마십니다.

I love drinking beer especially **Belgian beer**.
벨기에 맥주를 특히 즐겨 마십니다.

I enjoy the **finger food** there.
거기 안주를 즐깁니다.

바 또는 펍에서 하는 활동

I often go to Korean style bars **with my friend** to hang out.
저는 친구들과 어울려 한국식 바에 자주 갑니다.

We **have a chat over beer and soju**.
맥주와 소주를 마시며 대화를 나눕니다.

I sometimes go to a western style bar with my sister to **play darts and pool**.
여동생과 서양식 바에도 가끔 가서 다트, 포켓볼을 치기도 합니다.

We have a **chat and play darts** or **pool over beer**.
맥주를 마시며 대화를 나누고 다트나 포켓볼을 칩니다.

Useful Expressions

바 또는 펍 소개
on Friday night
on Saturdays
almost every weekend
whenever have time

좋아하는 음료 및 스낵
signature dishes
homemade burger
freshly cut fries
BBQ rib

함께 가는 사람
alone
by myself
with my friends
with my brother
with my sister
with my clients

바 또는 펍에서 하는 활동
enjoy homemade beer
drink imported liquor
watch a sport game

eat cheap wings
celebrate special days
talk about work
share personal thoughts

watch games
enjoy a ladies night
have special dishes

like to meet different people
can relieve stress

How to Answer

Q1. Describe the bar that you go to most often.

내용구성하기
- **Introduction**: ☑ 자주가는 바 또는 펍 소개
- **Body**: ☑ 음료 및 스낵   ☑ 좋아하는 이유
- **Closing**: ☑ 느낌 및 의견

Introduction
자주가는 바위 위치 & 함께 가는 사람 I often go to a western style bar near Gangnam subway station with my friends.

Body
음료 및 스낵 They have many kinds of beer and cocktails. Also, they serve great snacks and finger food. I think their small hotdogs are especially delicious.

좋아하는 이유① 분위기 I like the food and the mood at the bar. Whenever I go there, I enjoy some snacks over beer.

좋아하는 이유② 서비스 Moreover, the bartenders there are very friendly. Even if I visit alone, I feel comfortable and enjoy talking to them. For those reasons, I often go to that bar.

Closing
느낌 및 의견 That Western style bar is one of my favorite places to go for a drink.

친구들과 강남역 근처에 있는 서양식 바에 종종 갑니다. 다양한 종류의 맥주와 칵테일이 나오고 간식 및 안주도 좋습니다. 특히 작은 핫도그가 맛있습니다. 저는 바에서 나오는 음식과 분위기를 좋아합니다. 그곳에 갈 때마다 맥주와 안주를 즐겨먹습니다. 또 바텐더들이 아주 친절합니다. 혼자 가더라도 맘이 편해서 그들과 대화를 즐겁게 나누지요. 이런 이유에서 그 술집에 가는 것을 좋아합니다. 서양식 스타일의 바는 한잔하러 갈 때 가장 좋아하는 장소 중 하나입니다.

바/펍 가기 에서는 주로 자주 가는 바/펍 묘사, 바/펍에서 주로 하는 활동, 최근에 바/펍에 간 경험 등의 문제가 출제되니 당황하지 않도록 예상질문에 대한 답변을 미리 준비하도록 합니다.

Q2. Tell me about a memorable incident that happened at a bar.

내용구성하기	Introduction	☑ 기억에 남는 바 소개	
	Body	☑ 사건 배경	☑ 사건 결말
	Closing	☑ 느낌 및 의견	

Introduction

기억에 남는 바 소개 I will tell you about one of the most memorable incidents I have had at a bar. I often go to a bar that is located in Gangnam.

Body

사건 배경 Last year, I went to the bar with my friends. We ate some finger food and played darts. We had a really great time. We stayed there for about 3 hours. After hanging out, we left together.

사건 결말 After a few minutes, I realized that I had left my mobile phone at the bar. I quickly went back to the bar and fortunately, I found my phone.

Closing

느낌 및 의견 From this experience, I learned to check my belongings carefully before leaving.

술집에서 있었던 가장 기억나는 사건을 얘기해보겠습니다. 저는 강남에 있는 한 술집에 자주 갑니다. 작년에 친구들과 함께 그곳에 갔었죠. 안주도 먹고 다트 게임도 하며 즐거운 시간을 보냈습니다. 약 3시간 정도 있었습니다. 재밌게 즐기고 술집을 떠났습니다. 그런데 몇 분 후에 핸드폰을 그 술집에 두고 온 것을 깨달았습니다. 재빨리 그 술집으로 돌아갔는데 다행히 핸드폰을 찾을 수 있었습니다. 그 경험 덕분에 자리를 뜨기 전에 소지품을 확인하는 습관을 갖게 됐습니다.

취미나 관심사를 그룹으로 즐기는 것을 좋아한다면 그에 따른 1) 즐기는 이유 2) 관심을 갖게 된 계기 3) 경험 등을 혼자 즐기는 상황과 다른 특징들을 생각하여 답변을 구성하는 것이 효과적입니다. 이야기를 서술하듯 누구와 함께, 언제, 어디에서 등과 관련된 정보를 구체적으로 언급하면서 취미생활에 대한 자신의 느낌이나 의미를 설명하면 훌륭한 답변이 될 수 있습니다.

 **My Answer** — Use the expressions in the Skill Up section to develop your sentences.

- Introduction

- Body

- Closing

OPIc
도전! IM+

UNIT **8**

공원가기

UNIT 08 공원가기

OPIc 도전! IM+

Learning Objectives

자주가는 공원에 대해 묘사하고 공원에서 주로 하는 활동, 공원에서 있었던 기억에 남는 경험 등을 말할 수 있다.

Frequently Asked Questions

- Please tell me about a park that you go to often.
- How often do you go to the park? What do you usually do at the park?
- Please tell me about a memorable experience you had at a park.
- What kind of things do you take when you go to a park?
- Are there any issues or concerns you see with parks and their facilities?

Brainstorming

Step 1 Brainstorm key words and expressions about the topic.
Step 2 Use the words and expressions to brainstorm possible questions.

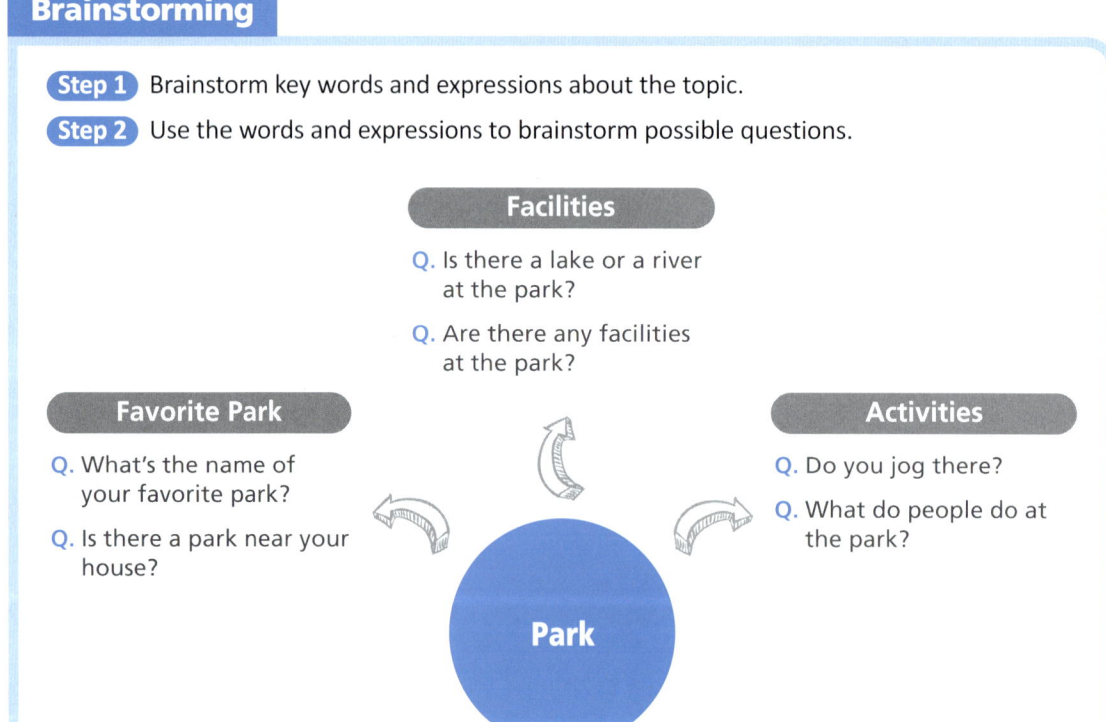

Facilities
Q. Is there a lake or a river at the park?
Q. Are there any facilities at the park?

Favorite Park
Q. What's the name of your favorite park?
Q. Is there a park near your house?

Activities
Q. Do you jog there?
Q. What do people do at the park?

Park

Skill up! Expressions

Useful Expressions

공원 소개

There is a park **near my apartment** building called Seoho Park.
제가 사는 아파트 근처에 서호 공원이란 곳이 있습니다.

It is about 10 minutes from my house **on foot**.
집에서 도보로 약 10분 거리에 있습니다.

My favorite park is Central Park near my house.
제가 가장 좋아하는 공원은 집 근처에 있는 센트럴 파크입니다.

It is a national park **located** near Seoul.
서울 근처에 있는 국립 공원이지요.

공원 소개
back of my office
close to the river
next to a community center
in front of my house

by bus
by subway
by car
by train
by taxi

situated
placed
found

공원 시설 및 분위기

There is a lake in the middle of the park.
공원 한가운데에 호수가 있습니다.

There are many **benches** and **exercise equipment** around the lake.
호수 주변에는 벤치와 운동 시설들이 많이 있습니다.

The park is very **clean**.
공원은 아주 깨끗합니다.

The park is very crowded on the weekend.
주말에는 공원이 사람들로 붐빕니다.

공원 시설 및 분위기
campground
tennis court
ball park
jogging track
trekking path
trees
resting area
dog park

full of green
energetic
not polluted

quiet | relaxing | stress-relieving | sophisticated

공원에서 하는 활동

I often go to the park to **exercise**.
운동하러 공원에 자주 갑니다.

I go jogging in the park every morning.
매일 아침 공원에서 조깅을 합니다.

I go on a picnic in the park with my family on the weekend.
주말에 가족과 공원에서 피크닉을 합니다.

공원에서 하는 활동
walk | run | hike | jog | trek | camp | stroll

walk my dog
ride a bike
take a walk
play frisbee
read books
listen to music

baseball | soccer | basketball | catch

How to Answer

Q1. Please tell me about a park that you go to often.

내용구성하기
- **Introduction** ☑ 공원 소개
- **Body** ☑ 시설 ☑ 주변환경 ☑ 공원에서 했던 일
- **Closing** ☑ 느낌 및 의견

Introduction
`공원 소개` I will tell you about a park near my house. It is called Central Park.

Body
`시설` There are many facilities, like exercise equipment, comfortable benches, soccer fields, and badminton courts. I often see many people using them.

`주변환경` Also, there are famous restaurants and cafes near the park.

`공원에서 했던 일` Last weekend, I had Chinese milk tea at one of the cafes. It is one of the biggest parks in my city.

Closing
`느낌 및 의견` I think it is a good place to exercise and relax.

집 근처에 있는 센트럴 파크란 공원에 대해 얘기해보겠습니다. 운동시설, 편안한 벤치, 축구장, 배드민턴 코트같은 시설들이 많이 있습니다. 많은 사람들이 그 시설들을 이용합니다. 또한 공원 근처에는 유명한 레스토랑과 카페가 있습니다. 지난 주에는 한 카페에서 중국식 밀크티를 마셨습니다. 우리 도시에서 가장 큰 공원중에 하나입니다. 운동하거나 휴식하기에 좋은 장소입니다.

공원 가기는 야외 여가활동으로 많이 선호하는 항목입니다. 이와 관련하여 공통되는 표현들을 익혀두면 보다 효율적으로 답변할 수 있습니다. 대표적인 문항유형으로는 1) 패턴(즐기는 빈도와 함께 동행하는 사람 및 장소묘사), 2) 야외활동을 즐기는 이유 및 계기(기억에 남는 경험), 3) 야외활동 할 때 챙겨가는 물건 등에 대한 질문이 있습니다. 이야기를 서술하듯 구체적으로 답변하는 연습이 필요합니다

Q2. How often do you go to the park? What do you usually do at the park?

내용구성하기	Introduction	☑ 자주가는 공원 소개	
	Body	☑ 공원 주변 묘사	☑ 공원에서 하는 활동
	Closing	☑ 느낌 및 의견	

Introduction

자주가는 공원 소개 I often go to a park called Olympic Park with my wife on the weekend. It takes about 10 minutes by foot from our home.

Body

공원 주변 묘사 There is a big lake in the center of the park. Also, there are many flowers and trees.

공원에서 하는 활동① I like walking along the lake and taking pictures there.

공원에서 하는 활동② As I mentioned, I spend time at the park with my wife. It's a good chance to have a conversation with her.

공원에서 하는 활동③ On the left side of the lake, there are public exercise equipment. I sometimes exercise there. I feel refreshed after exercising.

Closing

느낌 및 의견 I can relax and exercise for free at the park. It is a great place.

저는 주말에 아내와 함께 올림픽 공원에 자주 갑니다. 집에서 도보로 약 10분 거리에 있는 곳입니다. 공원 한가운데는 큰 호수가 있습니다. 꽃과 나무도 아주 많습니다. 저는 호수 주변을 따라 산책하고 사진 찍는 것을 좋아합니다. 앞서 말했듯이, 공원에서는 아내와 함께 시간을 보냅니다. 대화를 나눌 수 있는 좋은 기회지요. 호수 왼쪽에는 공용 운동 시설이 있습니다. 가끔 거기서 운동을 합니다. 운동하면 기분 전환이 되는 것을 느끼지요. 공원에서는 돈을 들이지 않고도 여유롭게 휴식과 운동을 즐길 수 있죠. 멋진 장소입니다.

고득점 tip!

공원에서 주로 하는 일이 무엇인지, 자주 가는 공원에는 무엇이 있는지 등의 문제가 출제 됩니다. 공원에 대해 묘사할 때, 가운데에 호수가 있다면 'On the right side of the lake…', 'On the left side of the lake…' 등의 표현으로 기준점을 잡고 묘사 대상의 위치를 설명하면서 말하는 것이 좋습니다.

My Answer — Use the expressions in the Skill Up section to develop your sentences.

- Introduction

- Body

- Closing

OPIc
도전! IM+

UNIT 9
해변가기

UNIT 09 해변가기

Learning Objectives

내가 알고 있는 해변을 소개하고 해변에서 하는 활동, 해변을 좋아하는 이유 등을 말할 수 있다.

Frequently Asked Questions

- How often do you go to the beach? Who do you usually go with?
- How do you get to the beach and what do you take with you?
- What kind of things do you usually do at the beach? Do you sunbathe or swim? Tell me about them in detail.
- What kind of clothes do you usually wear when you go to the beach? Describe your favorite beachwear in detail.

Brainstorming

Step 1 Brainstorm key words and expressions about the topic.
Step 2 Use the words and expressions to brainstorm possible questions.

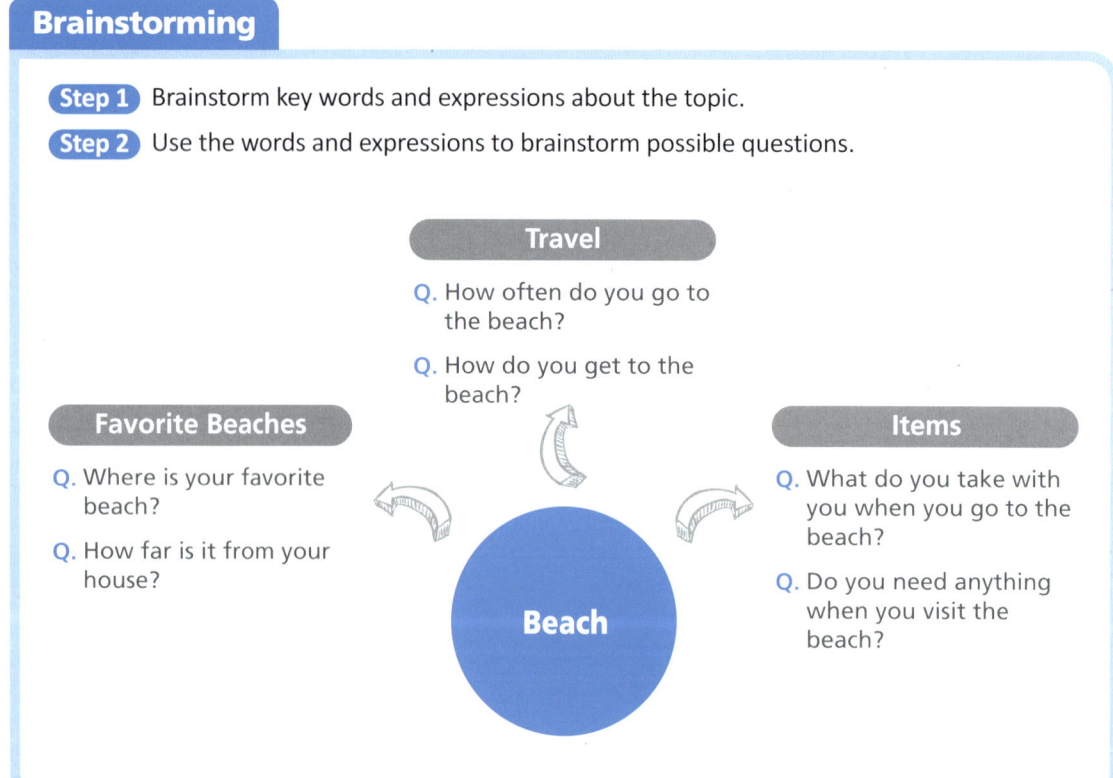

Travel
Q. How often do you go to the beach?
Q. How do you get to the beach?

Favorite Beaches
Q. Where is your favorite beach?
Q. How far is it from your house?

Items
Q. What do you take with you when you go to the beach?
Q. Do you need anything when you visit the beach?

Beach

Skill up! Expressions

해변 소개
I like Haeundae beach in Busan.
전 부산의 해운대 해변을 좋아합니다.

I enjoy going to Sokcho Beach.
전 속초 해변에 가는 것을 좋아합니다.

해변에 가기
I go to my favorite beach **once or twice a month**.
한 달에 한두 번 좋아하는 해변에 갑니다.

I go to the beach at least **three times a year**.
일년에 적어도 세번은 해변에 갑니다.

I usually drive to the beach.
보통 해변까지 운전을 해서 갑니다.

I take the train to the beach.
기차를 타고 해변에 갑니다.

공원에서 하는 활동
I like **playing in the water**.
물속에서 노는 것을 좋아합니다.

I enjoy **walking along the beach**.
해변을 따라 산책하는 것을 좋아합니다.

I always **go to the fish market near the beach**.
해변 근처에 있는 수산물 시장에 항상 갑니다.

해변이 좋은 이유
I like the beach because **it is clean and beautiful**.
그 해변이 깨끗하고 아름다워서 좋아합니다.

It has **clear water and a wide sand beach**.
해변의 바닷물이 깨끗하고 모래사장이 넓습니다.

Useful Expressions

해변 소개
I usually go to
the beach I love to go to is
I mostly want to go to

I am fond of
I love
I like
what do when I have free time is

해변가기
once a day
twice a week
three times a month
take a bus
take subway
take an express train

해변에서 하는 활동
swimming in the water
seeing a lot of marine life
drinking beer
watching the night sky
tanning

visit a small island
participate in activities
find the best site for diving
have seafood

해변이 좋은 이유
I can enjoy swimming
I like to watch the sea
it helps me relieve stress

beautiful white sand
unique geography
convenient infrastructure
different kinds of sea animals

How to Answer

Q1. Tell me about your favorite beach.

내용구성하기	Introduction	☑ 자주가는 해변 소개
	Body	☑ 좋아하는 이유 3가지
	Closing	☑ 느낌 및 의견

Introduction

(자주가는 해변 소개) I'll tell you about my favorite beach. My favorite beach is Haeundae in Busan. I like going to the beach, even though it's a bit far from my house.

Body

(좋아하는 이유① 풍경) It is a wide sand beach, so the scenery of the beach is very beautiful.

(좋아하는 이유② 음식) Also, there are many delicious seafood restaurants along the beach. I especially like eating prawns and crabs there.

(좋아하는 이유③ 사람들) Moreover, people there are very friendly to tourists.

Closing

(느낌 및 의견) I think it is one of the most beautiful beaches in Korea.

제가 가장 좋아하는 해변을 말씀 드리겠습니다. 제가 가장 좋아하는 해변은 부산의 해운대입니다. 집에서 멀리 떨어져 있음에도 불구하고 그 해변에 가는 것을 좋아합니다. 넓은 모래 사장이 펼쳐져 있어서 해변의 경치가 아주 아름답습니다. 또한 해변 근처에 맛있는 해산물 레스토랑이 많이 있습니다. 그곳에서 새우와 게를 먹는 것을 특히 좋아합니다. 게다가 관광객들에게 아주 친절한 곳입니다. 한국에서 가장 아름다운 해변 중 한 곳이라고 생각합니다.

답변 tip!

해변 가기, 캠핑하기 및 공원 가기 등의 항목은 야외 여가 활동으로 분류됩니다. 이와 관련하여 공통되는 표현들을 익혀두면 보다 효율적으로 답변할 수 있습니다. 대표적인 문항유형으로는 1) 패턴(즐기는 빈도와 함께 동행하는 사람 및 장소묘사), 2) 야외활동을 즐기는 이유 및 계기(기억에 남는 경험), 3) 야외활동 할 때 챙겨가는 물건 등에 대한 질문이 있습니다.

Q2. How do you get to the beach and what do you take with you?

내용구성하기
- Introduction ☑ 자주가는 해변 소개
- Body ☑ 해변에 가는 방법   ☑ 해변에 가지고 가는 물건
- Closing ☑ 느낌 및 의견

Introduction
자주가는 해변 소개 When I have time, I go to my favorite beach, Mangsang, with my wife.

Body
해변에 가는 방법 I usually drive there because then I don't have to make plans in advance. It takes about 4 hours by car. I sometimes take the train to get there. There is a bullet train from my town to the beach. It only takes 3 hours and I can enjoy the scenery from the train.

해변에 가지고 가는 물건 I just take a few items with me when I go to the beach. They are my phone, sunglasses, and a beach towel. I can take pictures and listen to music using my phone. Also, I always wear sunglasses at the beach. Lastly, I enjoy playing in the water, so I need to take a beach towel.

Closing
느낌 및 의견 Those are the things I usually take when I go to the beach.

시간이 생기면 아내와 함께 가장 좋아하는 해변인 망상 해수욕장에 갑니다. 대부분 차로 운전해서 가는데 미리 계획을 세울 필요가 없기 때문입니다. 자가용으로 약 4시간 정도 걸립니다. 가끔은 기차를 타고 가기도 합니다. 우리 동네에서 해변까지 가는 고속열차가 있습니다. 3시간 밖에 안 걸리는데, 기차에서 경치를 감상할 수 있습니다. 해변에 갈 때는 몇 가지만 챙겨 갑니다. 휴대폰, 선글라스 그리고 비치 타월입니다. 휴대폰으로 사진을 찍고 음악 감상을 할 수 있지요. 해변에서는 선글라스를 낍니다. 물 속에서 노는 것을 좋아하기 때문에 비치 타월을 갖고 가야 합니다. 보통 이런 것들을 해수욕장에 갈 때 들고 갑니다.

고득점 tip!
야외 여가 활동과 관련된 주제의 질문들로 어떤 물건을 가져갈 것인지에 대한 질문이 자주 등장하는데, 가져갈 물건을 3~4개 정도 나열한 후 그 물건을 가져가는 이유 및 그 물건의 용도 등을 함께 설명하면 풍부한 답변을 완성할 수 있습니다.

 **Use the expressions in the Skill Up section to develop your sentences.**

— Introduction

— Body

— Closing

OPIc 도전! IM+

UNIT 10

음악 감상하기

UNIT 10 음악 감상하기

OPIc 도전 IM+

Learning Objectives

내가 좋아하는 음악 장르 및 가수, 음악을 좋아하는 이유 등에 대해 말할 수 있다.

Frequently Asked Questions

- What kind of music do you like best? Who is your favorite singer?
- When and where do you usually listen to music?
- What device do you use to listen to music?
- Have you had a memorable experience while listening to music?
- What changes have there been from the past until now in the music style that you like?

Brainstorming

Step 1 Brainstorm key words and expressions about the topic.
Step 2 Use the words and expressions to brainstorm possible questions.

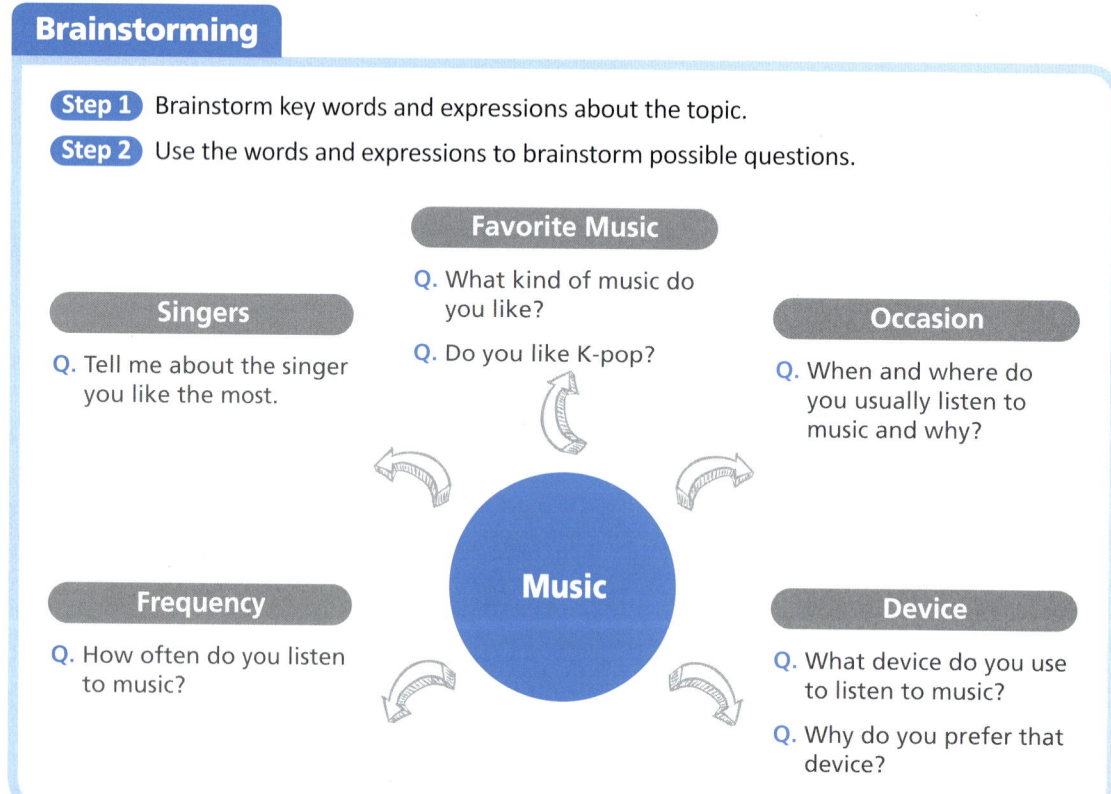

Favorite Music
Q. What kind of music do you like?
Q. Do you like K-pop?

Singers
Q. Tell me about the singer you like the most.

Occasion
Q. When and where do you usually listen to music and why?

Frequency
Q. How often do you listen to music?

Device
Q. What device do you use to listen to music?
Q. Why do you prefer that device?

Music

Skill up! Expressions

Useful Expressions

좋아하는 음악 장르 및 가수

I like **hip-hop music** the best.
저는 힙합 음악을 가장 좋아합니다.

I enjoy listening to **classical music**.
전 클래식 음악 감상을 좋아합니다.

My favorite singer is Radiohead.
가장 좋아하는 가수는 라디오헤드입니다.

I like him because of his voice.
그를 좋아하는 이유는 목소리 때문입니다.

좋아하는 음악장르
soundtracks | pop music |
rap music | live music |
heavy metal |
dance music | classical music |
rhythm and blues

음악 듣기

I usually listen to music **when I commute**.
출퇴근길에 주로 음악을 듣습니다.

I listen to music **on the bus**.
버스에서 음악을 듣습니다.

I always listen to classical music **before going to bed**.
잠자기 전에 클래식 음악을 항상 듣습니다.

I use my smart phone to listen to music.
스마트폰을 사용해 음악을 듣습니다.

I play music on **my car radio**.
자동차 라디오로 음악을 틉니다.

There are many **music apps**.
음악 앱이 많이 있습니다.

음악감상 방법
while I'm on my way somewhere
while I commute to work
before I go to sleep
while I'm cleaning
when I feel gloomy
when I feel down
when I read a book
when I find it hard to concentrate

음악이 좋은 이유

Classical music is very **relaxing**.
클래식 음악은 마음을 편안하게 해줍니다.

I like old pop music because it makes me **feel happy**.
전 들으면 행복하기 때문에 올드팝을 좋아합니다.

It **cheers me up**.
힘이 납니다.

음악을 즐기는 이유 및 감상
enjoyable | joyful | delightful |
cheerful | lively | uplifting |
relaxing | relieved | relaxed |
calm | comfort | entertaining |
amusing | consoled | comforted |
feel better | improve my mood

How to Answer

Q1. What kinds of music do you like? Who is your favorite singer?

내용구성하기	Introduction	☑ 좋아하는 장르	
	Body	☑ 좋아하는 가수	☑ 가수 특징
	Closing	☑ 느낌 및 의견	

Introduction

좋아하는 음악 장르 I listen to many kinds of music, but my favorite is ballads.

Body

좋아하는 가수 My favorite singer is Sung Si-Kyung. His ballad songs are famous and popular in Korea. Among his songs, I love "On the street" the most.

가수 특징 He has a sweet voice. I listen to his songs while commuting or before going to bed. They make me feel relaxed.

Closing

느낌 및 의견 I'm planning to go to his concert next month.

다양한 종류의 음악을 듣는데 가장 좋아하는 건 발라드입니다. 제일 좋아하는 가수는 성시경입니다. 그의 발라드 곡은 한국에서 유명하고 인기가 많습니다. 그의 노래 중 "거리에서"를 제일 좋아합니다. 그의 목소리는 감미롭습니다. 통근 길이나 잠자기 전에 그의 노래를 듣습니다. 노래를 들으면 긴장이 풀립니다. 다음 달에 그의 콘서트에 갈 계획입니다.

음악감상하기는 취미나 관심사 주제 중 가장 많이 선택하는 항목 중 하나입니다. 자주 출제되는 질문 유형으로는 1) 패턴(언제, 어디에서, 즐기는 빈도), 2) 좋아하는 장르, 3) 특별히 기억에 남는 일화(관심을 갖게 된 계기, 관심의 변화 및 본인에게 끼친 영향) 등이 있습니다.

Q2. What device do you use to listen to music?

내용구성하기	Introduction	☑ 음악을 듣는 장비	☑ 음악을 듣는 장소
	Body	☑ 즐겨 듣는 음악 장비	☑ 장비 사용의 이유
	Closing	☑ 느낌 및 의견	

Introduction
장비 및 장소 소개 I usually listen to music using my phone. I often listen to music on the bus when I commute.

Body
즐겨 듣는 음악 장비 I used to use an MP3 player or a CD player but I mostly use my phone these days.

이유 ① 편리성 First of all, my smartphone is a very convenient way to listen to music. It's very portable and I take it with me wherever I go.

이유 ② 유용성 Moreover, it can store hundreds of music files. Also, there are many consumer-friendly music apps.

Closing
느낌 및 의견 So it's a very useful device to listen to music and I use it every single day.

주로 휴대폰으로 음악을 듣습니다. 통근 길에 버스에서 음악을 자주 듣습니다. 전에는 MP3 플레이어나 CD 플레이어를 사용했는데 요새는 거의 휴대폰을 사용합니다. 스마트폰은 아주 편리한 음악감상 방식입니다. 일단 휴대하기가 편하니까 어딜 가나 갖고 다니지요. 또 수백 개의 음악 파일을 저장할 수 있습니다. 또한 고객 편의적인 음악 앱들이 많이 있습니다. 그래서 스마트폰은 음악 듣기에 아주 유용한 장치이지요, 매일매일 사용합니다.

고득점 tip!

음악 관련하여 최근 자주 나오는 문제(음악을 듣기 기기)의 유형을 파악하여 미리 준비하는 것이 중요합니다. 좋아하는 음악 장르나 음악 기기 묘사등의 문제가 나올 수 있으니 질문을 잘 듣고 알맞은 답변을 하도록 합니다.

 **Use the expressions in the Skill Up section to develop your sentences.**

— Introduction

— Body

— Closing

OPIc
도전! IM+

UNIT 11
조깅/걷기

UNIT 11 조깅/걷기

OPIc 도전! IM+

Learning Objectives

평소 조깅하는 장소를 소개하고, 조깅/걷기의 장점 및 주의점 등에 대해 말할 수 있다.

Frequently Asked Questions

- Please tell me about a place you like to go jogging. Where is it?
- Why do you enjoy jogging? What are the advantages of jogging?
- What do you do to prevent injuries when jogging?
- What do you usually take with you when you go jogging/walking?
- What clothes or shoes do you normally wear when you go jogging/walking?

Brainstorming

Step 1 Brainstorm key words and expressions about the topic.
Step 2 Use the words and expressions to brainstorm possible questions.

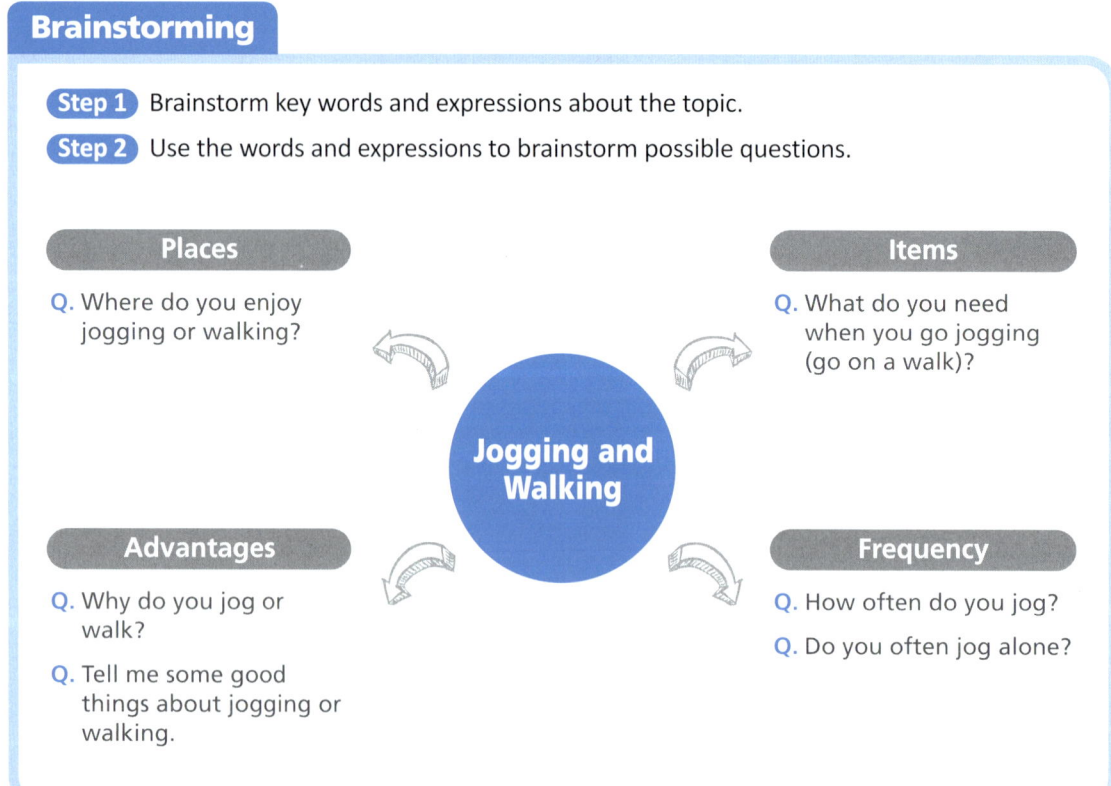

Places
Q. Where do you enjoy jogging or walking?

Items
Q. What do you need when you go jogging (go on a walk)?

Advantages
Q. Why do you jog or walk?
Q. Tell me some good things about jogging or walking.

Frequency
Q. How often do you jog?
Q. Do you often jog alone?

Skill up! Expressions

Useful Expressions

조깅/걷기 하는 장소 소개

I often go to **a park** near my house to jog.
집 근처 공원에 조깅하러 자주 갑니다.

There is **a nice jogging path** in the park.
공원 안에 좋은 조깅 코스가 있습니다.

I enjoy walking along a river **in my neighborhood**.
동네에 있는 강을 따라 산책하는 것을 좋아합니다.

I prefer to jog at the park **next to my apartment**.
아파트 옆에 있는 공원에서 조깅하는 것을 선호합니다.

조깅/걷기 하는 장소 소개
river | community stadium | gym | schoolyard

well-paved jogging track
new walking path
wide tracks
safe path for walking

around a small mountain
along the lake
beside the river

조깅 / 걷기의 장점

Jogging is **a good cardio exercise**.
조깅은 좋은 유산소 운동입니다.

It is a good way to **stay in shape**.
건강을 유지하는 좋은 방법입니다.

I can **get fresh air** when I walk in the park.
공원에서 산책하면 신선한 공기도 마실 수 있습니다.

It is **easy** to do.
실천하기도 쉽지요.

It doesn't cost me anything.
전혀 돈이 들지 않습니다.

조깅/걷기 장점
perfect exercise
the best work-out

keep people healthy
lose weight
anywhere and anytime you want

necessary | essential | important | significant | meaningful

relieve stress and tension

주의 할 점

You should **wear comfortable clothes** when you go jogging.
조깅할 때는 편한 옷을 입어야 합니다.

You need to **wear proper running shoes**.
적절한 런닝화를 신어야 합니다.

You should **warm up** before jogging.
조깅하기 전에 준비운동을 해야 합니다.

주의할 점
keeping your eyes on the road
wear clothes that keep your body warm
wear sunscreen to protect your skin
put on shoes designed for jogging

www.carrotenglish.com

How to Answer

Q1. Please tell me about a place you like to go jogging. Where is it?
Please tell me about a place you like to go for a walk. Where is it?

내용구성하기	Introduction	☑ 조깅하는 장소		
	Body	☑ 특징	☑ 볼 수 있는 것	☑ 조깅후에 하는 일
	Closing	☑ 느낌 및 의견		

Introduction

주로 조깅 하는 장소 I usually go jogging at Suk-chon Lake Park on the weekend.

Body

특징 및 볼 수 있는 것들 There are two big lakes in the center of the park. I jog along the lakes and exercise there. The walking track around the lakes is really good for joggers. Also, there are many trees and flowers. When I jog there, I can experience nature.

조깅후에 하는 일 After jogging, I often go to a cafe next to the park. They have nice fresh juice.

Closing

느낌 및 의견 After jogging, I feel refreshed.

주말에는 석촌호수 공원에서 주로 조깅을 합니다. 공원 가운데 큰 호수가 2개 있습니다. 호수 주변을 따라 조깅을 하고 운동도 합니다. 호수 주변의 산책로가 조깅하는 사람들에게 아주 좋습니다. 나무와 꽃들도 많이 있습니다. 그곳에서 조깅을 하면 자연을 느낄 수 있습니다. 조깅 후에는 공원 근처에 카페에 갑니다. 카페에서는 신선한 주스를 판매합니다. 조깅을 하고 나면 기분이 상쾌해지죠.

답변 tip!

운동에 관한 다양한 설문항목 중 규칙적으로 즐길 수 있는 항목을 공통으로 준비하면 효율적입니다. 운동 관련한 질문 유형으로는 1) 운동패턴(얼마나 자주, 언제, 어디에서 하는지), 2) 즐겨가는 운동장소 묘사와 그 이유, 3) 즐기는 운동에 관심을 갖게 된 계기(운동을 하는 이유) 및 기억에 남는 경험(운동하는 방법 및 절차 포함) 등에 있습니다. 관련된 어휘와 표현을 익혀 답변을 구성해보도록 합니다.

Q2. Why do you enjoy jogging? What are the advantages of jogging?

내용구성하기	Introduction	☑ 조깅을 하는 이유
	Body	☑ 조깅의 좋은 점 3가지
	Closing	☑ 느낌 및 의견

Introduction
조깅을 하는 이유 I like jogging. It is good for my health.

Body
조깅의 좋은점 ① 다이어트 It is a good aerobic exercise. It is the cheapest way to lose weight.

조깅의 좋은점 ② 편의성 Also, it is easy to do. I didn't have to spend time or money learning how to do it. Other sports, like swimming and skiing, need practice. But jogging, you can start whenever you want.

조깅의 좋은점 ③ 건강 Additionally, it is good for blood circulation and prevents diseases, like diabetes and high blood pressure.

Closing
느낌 및 의견 Those are the advantages of jogging and the reasons why I enjoy it.

전 조깅을 좋아합니다. 건강에 좋은 운동이지요. 조깅은 훌륭한 유산소 운동입니다. 몸무게를 줄일 수 있는 가장 저렴한 방법이기도 합니다. 실천하기도 쉽습니다. 운동 방법을 배우기 위해 돈이나 시간을 쓸 필요가 없으니까요. 수영이나 스키 같은 다른 스포츠는 연습을 해야 하죠. 하지만 조깅은 언제라도 원할 때 시작할 수 있습니다. 게다가 혈액 순환에도 좋고 당뇨나 고혈압 같은 병도 예방해 줍니다. 이런 점이 조깅의 장점이고 제가 조깅을 즐기는 이유입니다.

고득점 tip!

조깅하기와 걷기는 서로 다른 설문조사 항목이지만 문제의 유형과 답변의 형태가 비슷하여 함께 준비하면 좀 더 효율적으로 학습할 수 있습니다. 경험을 물어보는 문제에 사실을 답하지 않아도 되므로 당황하지 말고 자연스럽게 스토리를 만들어 답변하도록 합니다.

My Answer — Use the expressions in the Skill Up section to develop your sentences.

– Introduction

– Body

– Closing

OPIc
도전! IM+

UNIT 12

국내 여행

UNIT 12 국내 여행

OPIc 도전! IM+

Learning Objectives

자신이 좋아하는 국내 여행지를 소개하고 최근 여행 경험 및 가장 기억에 남는 여행 등에 대해 이야기할 수 있다.

Frequently Asked Questions

- Where is your favorite place to visit in your country? Why do you like that place?
- When was the last time you traveled in your country?
- What do you pack when you go on a vacation in your country?
- What kind of things do you usually prepare before traveling?

Brainstorming

Step 1 Brainstorm key words and expressions about the topic.
Step 2 Use the words and expressions to brainstorm possible questions.

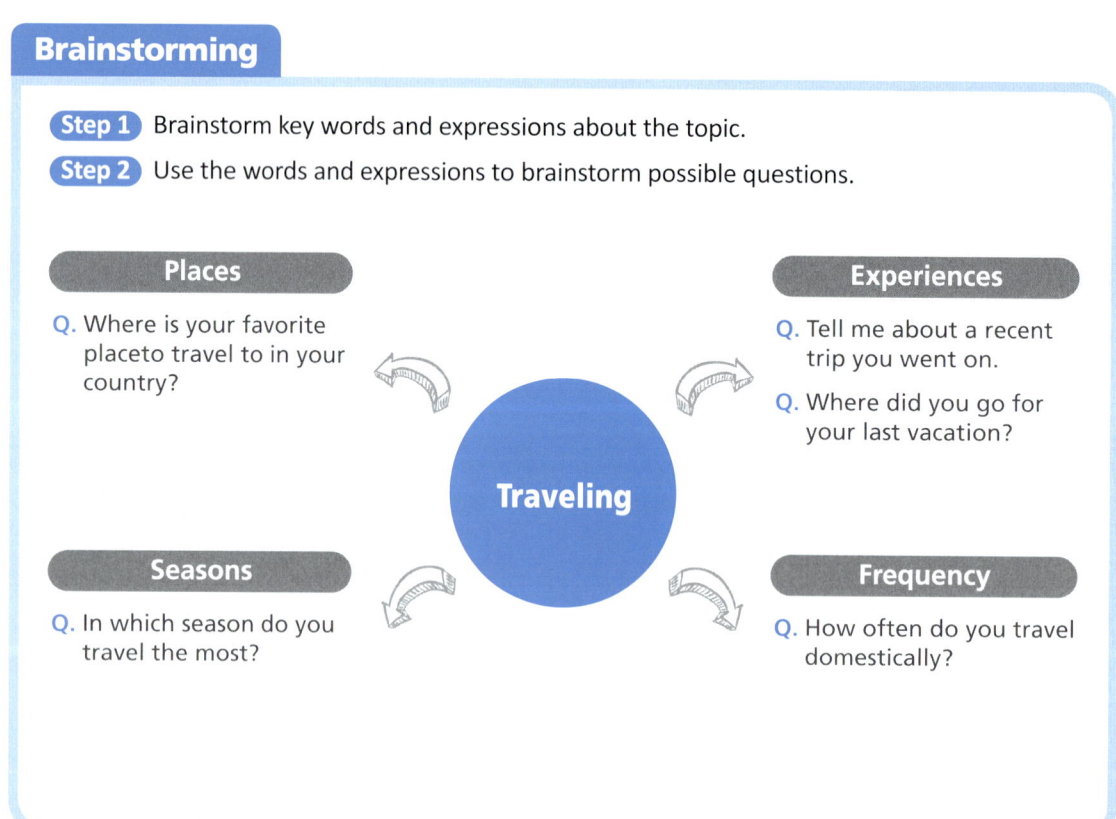

Places
Q. Where is your favorite place to travel to in your country?

Experiences
Q. Tell me about a recent trip you went on.
Q. Where did you go for your last vacation?

Seasons
Q. In which season do you travel the most?

Frequency
Q. How often do you travel domestically?

Skill up! Expressions

여행지 장소 소개

I enjoy traveling to Jeju Island with my family.
가족과 가는 제주도 여행을 좋아합니다.

I **sometimes** go to a beach **for my vacation**.
가끔 휴가 때 해수욕장에 갑니다.

I **often** travel to Busan with my friends.
친구들과 부산 여행을 자주 갑니다.

I go to **beaches** in Korea on my vacation.
휴가 때는 한국의 해수욕장에 갑니다.

여행가서 하는 활동

I spend time **visiting historical sites**.
역사적인 장소들을 방문합니다.

I love **trying local foods**.
현지 음식을 먹어보는 것도 좋아합니다.

I am a beach-goer; I always go to beaches while traveling.
전 해수욕을 좋아해서 여행할 때는 항상 해변에 갑니다.

여행 경험

I traveled to Busan with my family for a week last year.
작년에 가족과 일주일간 부산 여행을 했습니다.

I saw the **magnificent night view**.
야경이 정말 멋졌습니다.

I was thoroughly **impressed**.
아주 인상 깊은 경험이었습니다.

I had **a nice time** with my friends.
친구들과 즐거운 시간을 보냈습니다.

It was one of our best family vacations.
최고의 가족 휴가였습니다.

Useful Expressions

여행지 장소 소개
in my free time
on the weekend
during the holidays
at Christmas

sometimes | frequently | occasionally

mountains | lakes | valleys | camping sites | countryside | new cities | foreign countries

여행가서 하는 활동
taking a rest at the hotel
looking for delicious restaurants
making a new friends
visiting tourist attractions
experiencing new things

여행경험
impressive heritages
unique culture
interesting architecture

fascinated | amazed | surprised | touched | moved | afraid | overwhelmed

wished to visit there again
cannot forget about it
had very special moment

How to Answer

Q1. What is your favorite place to visit in your country? Why do you like that place?

내용구성하기	Introduction	☑ 좋아하는 여행지
	Body	☑ 좋아하는 이유 3가지
	Closing	☑ 느낌 및 의견

Introduction

좋아하는 여행지 I sometimes travel to Jeju Island.

Body

좋아하는 이유① 풍경 I like going there because of the nice scenery. It is a volcanic island. It is the only place in Korea where you can see gigantic granite rocks.

좋아하는 이유② 숙박시설 및 음식 Also, there are many good hotels and guesthouses. I usually stay at the Shilla Hotel. The local food is incredible. I especially love eating fresh seafood and pork there.

좋아하는 이유③ 환경 Moreover, there are many beautiful places to go like the wonderful beaches and Halla Mountain.

Closing

느낌 및 의견 It has beautiful natural sites and many good tourist attractions as well. It is one of the best tourist spots in Korea.

저는 가끔 제주도 여행을 갑니다. 거길 가는 이유는 풍경이 아름답기 때문입니다. 제주도는 화산섬입니다. 한국에서 유일하게 거대한 화강암 바위들을 볼 수 있는 곳이죠. 좋은 호텔과 게스트하우스도 많습니다. 저는 보통 신라 호텔에 묵습니다. 제주도 현지 음식은 정말 훌륭합니다. 특히 제주도의 신선한 해산물과 돼지고기를 좋아합니다. 아름다운 해변가와 한라산같이 아름다운 장소들이 많습니다. 아름다운 자연 지대와 관광 명소들도 다양합니다. 제주도는 한국에서 가장 훌륭한 관광 지역 중 한 곳입니다.

답변 tip!

국내여행의 대표적인 질문 유형으로는 1) (국내) 여행 장소 묘사하기, 2) (국내) 여행에서 하는 활동, 3) (국내) 여행을 보내는 방식에 관한 것입니다. 휴가를 보내는 목적 및 활동, 함께 보내는 사람 및 관련 경험 등 기본적인 사항에 대한 어휘와 표현을 익혀 답변을 미리 준비하도록 합니다.

Q2. Where do you like to go to on vacation in your country? Why do you like that place?

내용구성하기	Introduction	☑ 좋아하는 여행지
	Body	☑ 좋아하는 이유
	Closing	☑ 느낌 및 생각

Introduction

좋아하는 여행지 I like traveling in my country. There are many good places to visit in my country. Among them, I love visiting Busan the best.

Body

좋아하는 이유 ① 환경 It has lovely beaches and many tourist spots. Last year, I went to Haeundae Beach with my friends. The wide sand beach was crowded with people and was very lively.

좋아하는 이유 ② 음식 Also, the local food is really nice. For example, Busan is famous for seafood and milmyeon among many other dishes. I always go to the fish market in Busan to have fresh seafood. I have been there many times with family and friends. We have many good memories there.

Closing

느낌 및 의견 My family and I will travel to Busan again soon.

전 우리나라 여행을 좋아합니다. 우리나라에는 가볼 만한 곳들이 많습니다. 전 부산 여행을 가장 좋아합니다. 아름다운 해수욕장과 관광지들이 많이 있습니다. 작년에는 친구들과 해운대 해변에 갔습니다. 넓은 백사장이 인파로 붐볐는데 아주 활기가 넘쳤습니다. 현지 음식도 정말 맛있습니다. 예를 들면, 다른 음식들 중에서도 부산은 해산물과 밀면이 유명합니다. 저는 신선한 해산물을 사러 부산에 있는 수산물 시장에 항상 갑니다. 가족, 친구들과 그곳에 여러 번 갔었습니다. 부산에는 좋은 추억들이 많습니다. 가족과 조만간 다시 한번 부산에 갈 계획입니다.

고득점 tip!

콤보 문제의 유형으로 여행시 가지고 가는 물건에 대한 질문이 등장할 경우 먼저 가져갈 물건을 나열하고, 그 물건의 사용 목적을 차례대로 열거합니다. 이때, 현재시제를 사용하는 것에 주의하세요.

My Answer — Use the expressions in the Skill Up section to develop your sentences.

– Introduction

– Body

– Closing

UNIT 13

해외 여행

OPIc 도전! IM+

UNIT 13 해외 여행

OPIc 도전! IM+

Learning Objectives

기억에 남는 해외 여행지를 소개하고 사람들이 여행을 좋아하는 이유 및 여행시 고려사항 등에 대해 이야기 할 수 있다.

Frequently Asked Questions

- Where is the best place you've ever visited overseas?
- What activities do you enjoy when you travel?
- Which country or city do you want to travel to in the future?
- When you travel internationally, what do you usually eat? Tell me about the food you like to eat.
- Tell me about some changes in travel between the past and the present.

Brainstorming

Step 1 Brainstorm key words and expressions about the topic.
Step 2 Use the words and expressions to brainstorm possible questions.

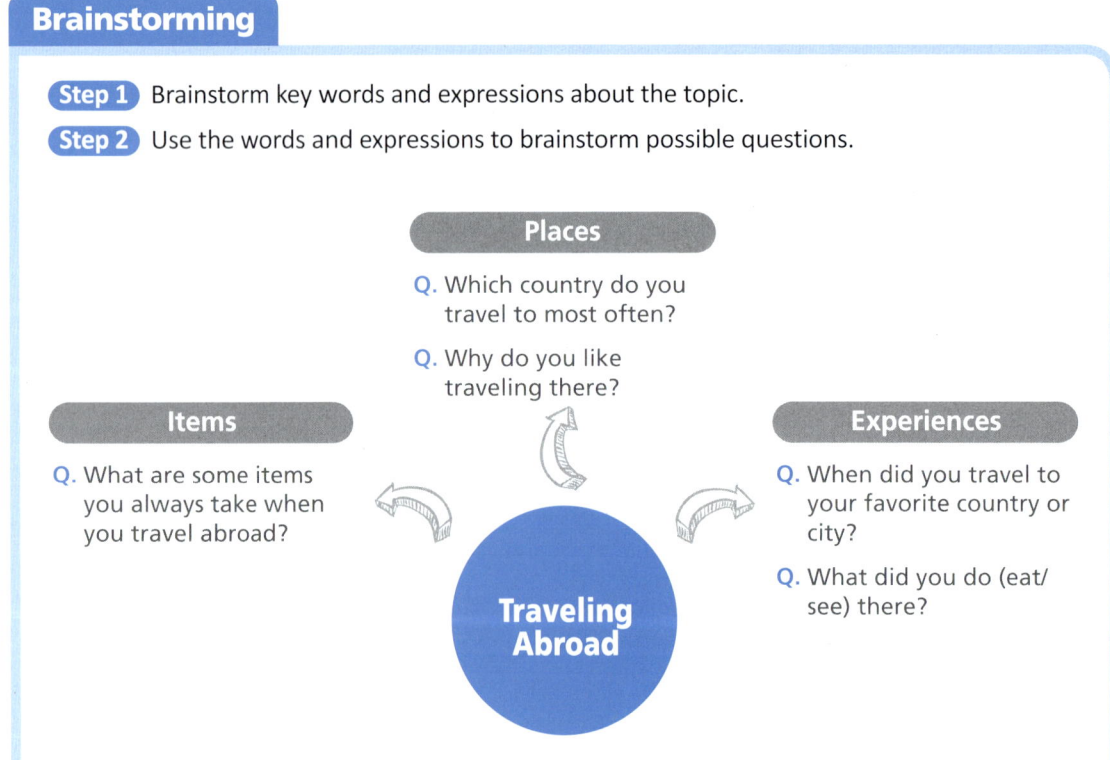

Places
Q. Which country do you travel to most often?
Q. Why do you like traveling there?

Items
Q. What are some items you always take when you travel abroad?

Experiences
Q. When did you travel to your favorite country or city?
Q. What did you do (eat/see) there?

Traveling Abroad

Skill up! Expressions

여행지 장소 소개

I **went on a three-week vacation** to Norway.
노르웨이로 3주간 휴가를 갔었습니다.

I recently went to London **for 9 days**.
최근 런던에 가서 9일간 있었습니다.

Last summer, I visited Hong Kong for the first time.
작년 여름 처음으로 홍콩을 방문했습니다.

여행가서 하는 활동

I like new experiences, so I try to **go to a different place each vacation**.
새로운 경험을 좋아해서 매번 휴가 때마다 다른 장소에 가려고 노력합니다.

When I go abroad on vacation, I **enjoy sightseeing**.
해외로 휴가를 가면 관광하는 것을 좋아합니다.

I like to buy presents for my friends.
친구들을 위한 선물을 사는 것을 좋아합니다.

I traveled **with a group** to Japan last year.
작년에는 일본으로 단체 여행을 갔습니다.

여행 경험

I **did volunteer work** in Cambodia, and it was an unforgettable experience.
캄보디아에서 자원봉사 활동을 했었는데 그건 잊지 못할 경험이었습니다.

The local people there were very friendly.
현지인들이 정말 친절했습니다.

I tried beef stew for the first time.
처음으로 소고기 스튜를 만들어 봤습니다.

I **saw a magnificent night view**.
정말 멋진 야경을 봤습니다.

It's breathtakingly beautiful.
숨막힐 정도로 아름다웠습니다.

Useful Expressions

여행기간
receive five days' annual vacation
go on a weekend retreat
travel for a year
take a short trip

여행 목적 및 활동
experience different cultures
sightsee around the country
try different foods
meet local people
take [go on] a city tour
visit the museum and arboretum
participate in a festival
take pictures
mingle with new people
go on a pub crawl
drop by a souvenir store

동행하는 사람
by myself
with my friends as well as my family

기억에 남는 경험
stay with a host family
travel by bicycle
travel on a student visa to America
tour around Europe
backpack through Africa

How to Answer

Q1. Where is the best place you've ever visited overseas? Why do you like the place?

내용구성하기	Introduction	☑ 여행지 소개
	Body	☑ 인상적인 점 3가지
	Closing	☑ 느낌 및 의견

Introduction

여행지 소개 I traveled to Italy 3 years ago. I stayed there for a week.

Body

인상적인 점① There is beautiful architecture and many interesting artifacts. When I walked into the Vatican, I was shocked by its scale and its history.

인상적인 점② In Italy, there are many amazing buildings, like the Leaning Tower of Pisa and the Duomo Church in Florence.

인상적인 점③ In addition, I enjoyed the local food. There I ate the best T-bone steak I've ever had.

Closing

느낌 및 의견 Italy is still the best place I have ever visited.

3년 전 이탈리아를 여행했습니다. 아름다운 건축물과 흥미로운 유물들이 많은 곳이지요. 바티칸에 들어갔을 때는 그 규모와 역사에 충격을 받았습니다. 이탈리아에는 피사의 사탑, 플로렌스의 두오모 성당 같은 멋진 건물들이 많습니다. 현지 음식도 좋았습니다. 이탈리아에서 먹은 티본 스테이크는 제가 먹었던 것 중 최고였습니다. 아직도 이탈리아는 제가 경험해본 최고의 장소입니다.

답변 tip!

해외여행의 대표적인 질문 유형으로는 1) (해외) 여행 장소 묘사하기, 2) (해외) 여행에서 하는 활동, 3) (해외) 여행을 보내는 방식에 관한 것입니다. 휴가를 보내는 목적 및 활동, 함께 보내는 사람 및 관련 경험 등 기본적인 사항에 대한 어휘와 표현을 익혀 답변을 미리 준비하도록 합니다.

Q2. Which country or city do you want to travel to in the future?

내용구성하기	Introduction	☑ 가고 싶은 여행지
	Body	☑ 가고 싶은 이유
	Closing	☑ 느낌 및 의견

Introduction

가고싶은 여행지 I want to travel to New Zealand and Iceland in the future.

Body

가고싶은 이유① These days, I feel stuffy because of the dirty air in Korea. There are too many cars and factories in Korea. Also, the country is very densely populated, so I want to experience nature and relax.

가고싶은 이유② One of my friends visited both countries 2 years ago. He showed me many breathtakingly beautiful pictures of his trip and told me interesting stories about his experiences traveling.

Closing

느낌 및 의견 If I visit New Zealand, I'll rent a camper and travel around with my wife.

나중에 뉴질랜드와 아이슬란드로 여행을 가보고 싶습니다. 요새 한국의 공기가 나빠서 답답하게 느껴집니다. 한국에는 자동차와 공장들이 너무 많습니다. 또한 인구도 너무 밀집돼 있고요. 그래서 자연을 느끼며 휴식하고 싶습니다. 친구 한 명이 2년 전에 두 개국을 모두 갔다 왔었는데, 너무나 아름다운 여행 사진들을 보여주며 여행 중에 겪은 재미난 얘기를 들려주더군요. 뉴질랜드에 가게 된다면 캠핑카를 빌려서 아내와 함께 여행을 다니려고 합니다.

고득점 tip!

해외여행 관련 질문 답변시 시제 사용에 주의해야 합니다. 경험에 대한 질문에 답할때는 과거 시제를 사용하고, 여행에서 하는 활동들에 대한 답변에는 현재시제를 사용합니다. 시제 사용만 잘 하여도 고득점을 받을 수 있는 좋은 방법 입니다.

My Answer — Use the expressions in the Skill Up section to develop your sentences.

- Introduction

- Body

- Closing

OPIc 도전! IM+

UNIT 14

집에서 보내는 휴가

UNIT 14 집에서 보내는 휴가

OPIc 도전! IM+

Learning Objectives

집에서 휴가를 보내는 이유에 대해 설명하고 집에서 하는 활동, 기억에 남는 경험 등을 이야기 할 수 있다.

Frequently Asked Questions

- What are some of your favorite indoor activities? If you stay home during your vacation, what do you do?
- Tell me about a memorable experience you had spending a vacation at home.
- When you spend your vacation at home, who do you spend your time with? What do you usually do with them?

Brainstorming

Step 1 Brainstorm key words and expressions about the topic.
Step 2 Use the words and expressions to brainstorm possible questions.

Experiences
Q. When was the last time you spent a vacation at home?
Q. What did you do?

Indoor Activities
Q. Do you enjoy watching TV at home?
Q. What is your favorite thing to do at home?

People
Q. Do you often spend time with your family?
Q. Do you sometimes invite your friends over to your house?

Vacation at Home

Skill up! Expressions

집에서 보내는 휴가
When I am on vacation, I just want to **relax at home**.
휴가는 그냥 집에서 쉬며 보내고 싶습니다.

I spend my vacations at home with family.
가족과 함께 집에서 휴가를 보냅니다.

I enjoy traveling but sometimes I also enjoy spending time at home.
여행을 좋아하지만 때로는 집에서 시간을 보내는 것도 좋아합니다.

집에서 보내는 휴가 중 하는 활동
My vacation is a **chance to spend time with my kids**.
휴가는 자녀들과 시간을 보낼 수 있는 기회입니다.

Vacation time is when I **catch up on household chores**.
휴가 기간은 밀린 집안 일을 하는 시기입니다.

During my vacation, I usually **read books and watch movies** at home.
휴가 기간 동안은 주로 집에서 책을 읽거나 영화를 봅니다.

I try to **cook some special food** for my family.
가족을 위해 특별한 요리를 만들어 봅니다.

I **catch up on sleep**.
밀린 잠을 보충합니다.

I **watch soap operas and TV shows** I missed while I was working.
일하느라 놓치고 못 봤던 드라마와 TV 프로를 봅니다.

I just **enjoy being alone and listening to music**.
혼자 있으면서 음악 듣는 것을 좋아합니다.

집에서 보내는 휴가 경험
It was my most **enjoyable** vacation ever.
이제까지 중 가장 즐거웠던 휴가였습니다.

I had a really **good time** with my kids.
아이들과 정말 좋은 시간을 보냈습니다.

I could **relieve all my stress** from work.
일하면서 받은 스트레스를 풀 수 있었습니다.

Useful Expressions

목적 및 활동
take a rest
have time to oneself
unwind
catch up on my sleep
reconnect with one's family
have people over for dinner
work on one's hobbies
run some errand
repair things

having a party
going to a movie
going outside
playing sports

집에서 보내는 휴가 경험
memorable | unforgettable | special | exciting | pleasant

forget about everything that bothered me
become even closer to each other
learn many things from it
think about myself and my future

How to Answer

Q1. What are some of your favorite indoor activities? If you stay home during your vacation, what do you do?

내용구성하기	Introduction	☑ 집에서 보내는 휴가의 즐거움
	Body	☑ 집에서 휴가를 보낼 때 하는 활동들 3가지
	Closing	☑ 느낌 및 의견

Introduction

집에서 보내는 휴가 I enjoy spending my vacation at home.

Body

활동①,② 영화보기/게임하기 I like the chance to relax and do many things I don't usually have time for. I enjoy spending time with my family. We spend time together watching movies and playing board games.

활동③ 요리하기 Sometimes we make special meals together, because we don't normally have time to cook. During vacation, I help my wife bake cookies or pies or we order in pizza or chicken and have a picnic at home.

Closing

느낌 및 의견 Staying home for vacation gives me time to unwind and reconnect with my family.

집에서 휴가를 보내는 것이 재미있습니다. 시간이 없어서 못했던 많은 일을 할 수 있고 쉴 수 있는 기회라서 좋습니다. 가족과 함께 지내는것도 좋습니다. 영화를 보거나 보드게임을 하면서 시간을 보냅니다. 때로는 다같이 특별한 음식을 만듭니다. 평소에는 요리할 시간이 없기 때문이죠. 휴가 기간에는 쿠키나 파이를 만드는 아내를 도와주거나 집에서 피자나 치킨을 시켜 먹습니다. 집에서 휴가를 보내면 가족과 함께 소통하며 여유를 즐길 수 있습니다.

답변 tip!

집에서 보내는 휴가의 대표적인 질문 유형으로는 1) 집에서 휴가를 보내는 이유 2) 집에서 휴가를 보낼 때 하는 활동, 3) 집에서 휴가를 보낸 경험에 관한 것입니다. 집에서 휴가를 보내는 목적 및 활동, 함께 보내는 사람 및 관련 경험 등 기본적인 사항에 대한 어휘와 표현을 익혀 답변을 미리 준비하도록 합니다.

Q2. When you spend your vacation at home, what do you usually do?

내용구성하기	Introduction	☑ 집에서 보내는 휴가
	Body	☑ 집에서 휴가를 보낼 때 하는 활동들 3가지
	Closing	☑ 느낌 및 의견

Introduction

집에서 보내는 휴가 I will tell you what I do when vacationing at home.

Body

활동① 휴식 The first thing I do is relax and try to do nothing but recover. This is because I am normally very busy at work.

활동② 수면 In addition, I sleep as much as I can. It is a great chance to catch up on sleep. When I work, I usually sleep less than 6 hours a night.

활동③ 집안일 접어두기 After that, I do some neglected housework. I sometimes push back doing my chores because I don't enjoy doing housework but after getting it out of the way, I feel refreshed.

Closing

느낌 및 의견 Those are the things I usually do while vacationing at home.

집에서 보내는 휴가에 대해 이야기해보겠습니다. 제가 제일 먼저 하는 일은 아무것도 하지 않고 쉬면서 회복하는 것입니다. 왜냐하면 평상시 직장에서 너무 바쁘기 때문입니다. 그리고 잘 수 있는 만큼 최대한 많이 잠을 잡니다. 모자랐던 잠을 보충하기 좋은 기회죠. 일할 때는 보통 하루 6시간도 자지 못합니다. 그 다음에는 미루어 뒀던 집안일을 합니다. 가사일 하는 것을 좋아하지 않아서 가끔 미뤄두는데 해치우고 나면 기분이 상쾌해집니다. 이런 일들이 보통 제가 집에서 휴가를 지낼 때 하는 일들입니다.

고득점 tip!

집에서 휴가를 보내는 이유 및 집에서 휴가를 보낼 때 하는 활동 등에 대한 문제가 등장할 때 이에 대해 상세히 서술하는 형태의 답변이 필요합니다. 구체적 예시와 함께 풍성한 답변을 미리 준비해 보도록 합니다. 집에서 보내는 휴가와 돌발질문으로 나오는 주말활동은 유사한 답변으로 활용이 가능하니 함께 준비해 보도록 합시다.

 **Use the expressions in the Skill Up section to develop your sentences.**

— Introduction

— Body

— Closing

II

실력다지기

☑ **Part 3 롤플레이**

Unit 15 | Eva에게 질문하기
Unit 16 | 전화로 질문하기
Unit 17 | 상황 설명하기
Unit 18 | 대안 제시하기

OPIc
도전!
IM+

OPIc 도전! IM+

UNIT 15

Eva에게 질문하기

UNIT 15

Eva에게 질문하기

OPIc 도전! IM+

Learning Objectives

상황과 주제를 이해하고 질문을 통해 면접관의 기호, 하는 일 및 활동 등 질문의 목적을 달성 할 수 있는 답변을 할 수 있다.

Frequently Asked Questions

- I live with my family. Please ask me 3 or 4 questions about my family.
- I often go to a park near my house. Please ask me 3 or 4 questions about the park I often visit.
- I went shopping with my sister last weekend. Ask me 3 or 4 questions about our shopping trip.
- I also like to spend my vacation at home. Ask me a couple of questions to find out about what I do to enjoy my vacation at home.

Brainstorming

Step 1 Brainstorm key words and expressions about the topic.
Step 2 Use the words and expressions to brainstorm possible questions.

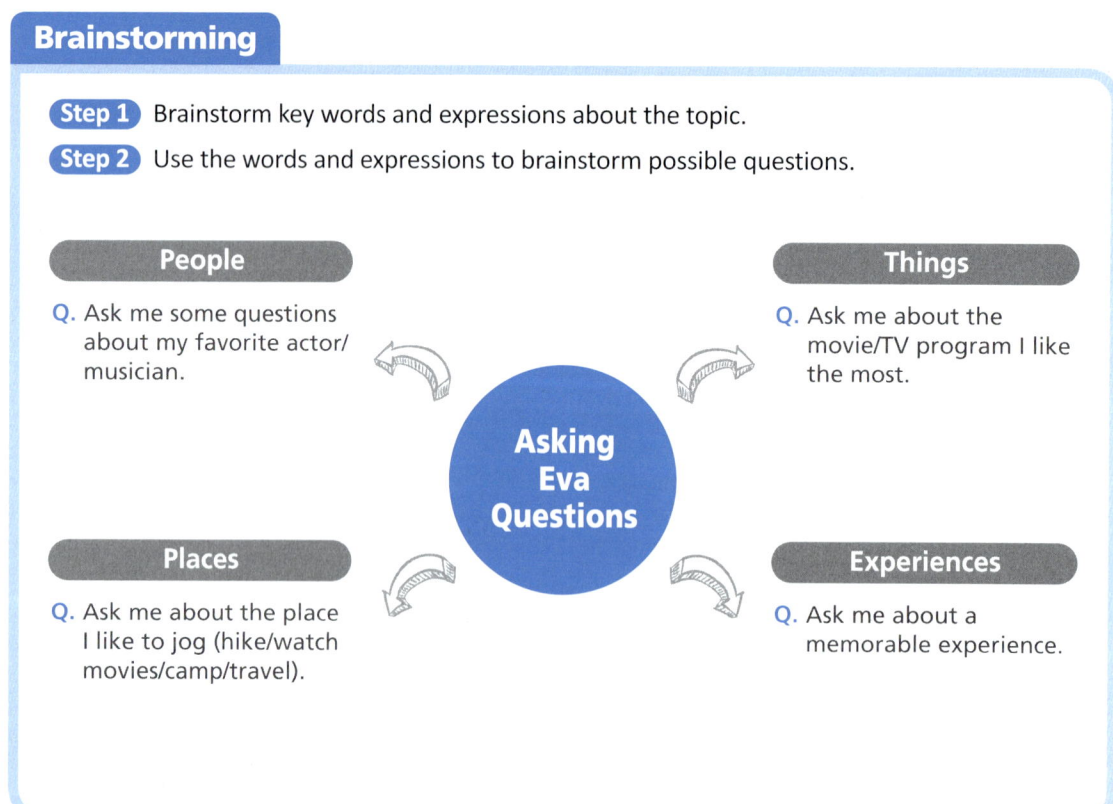

People
Q. Ask me some questions about my favorite actor/musician.

Things
Q. Ask me about the movie/TV program I like the most.

Places
Q. Ask me about the place I like to jog (hike/watch movies/camp/travel).

Experiences
Q. Ask me about a memorable experience.

Asking Eva Questions

Skill up! Expressions

질문 만들기 연습

There are four people in my family.
제 가족은 4명입니다.

▶ How many people are there in your family?
당신 가족은 몇 명입니까?

My wife is good at cooking.
제 아내는 요리를 잘 합니다.

▶ Is your wife good at cooking?
당신 아내는 요리를 잘합니까?

I sometimes go shopping with my family on the weekend.
가끔 주말에 가족과 쇼핑을 합니다.

▶ What do you do with your family on the weekend?
당신은 주말에 가족과 무엇을 합니까?

▶ Do you often go shopping with your family on the weekend?
당신은 주말에 가족과 쇼핑을 자주 갑니까?

I often go to a park near my house. It takes about 5 minutes to get there from my house by foot.
집 근처 공원에 자주 갑니다. 집에서 공원까지는 걸어서 5분 정도 걸립니다.

▶ How long does it take to get there from your house?
집에서 거기까지 가는데 얼마나 걸립니까?

I like listening to K-pop.
전 K팝을 즐겨 듣습니다.

▶ What kind of music do you like?
어떤 종류의 음악을 좋아합니까?

I go grocery shopping with my husband once a week.
일주일에 한번 남편과 장을 봅니다.

▶ How often do you go grocery shopping?
얼마나 자주 장을 봅니까?

I went to a bar with my co-workers yesterday.
어제 동료들과 술집에 갔습니다.

▶ What did you do yesterday?
어제 무엇을 했습니까?

▶ I am wondering what you did yesterday.
어제 당신이 무엇을 했는지 궁금합니다.

My best friend is James.
제 가장 친한 친구는 제임스입니다.

▶ What's your best friend's name?
당신의 가장 친한 친구 이름은 무엇입니까?

▶ Who's your best friend?
제일 친한 친구는 누구입니까?

Useful Expressions

인사말
hello, this is

질문하기
firstly
first off
first of all
the first thing is
the most
important thing is

can I ... ?
what do I need to ... ?
how do I arrange ... ?
how can I ... ?

lastly
at last
the final thing is

끝인사
your time
your help
your assistance
I appreciate

How to Answer

Q1. I live with my family. Please ask me 3 or 4 questions about my family.

내용구성하기	Introduction	☑ 인사말+질문 목적	
	Body	☑ 관련 이야기	☑ 질문 3가지
	Closing	☑ 마무리	

Introduction

인사말 +질문 목적 You told me you live with your family. If you don't mind, I'd like to ask a few questions about your family.

Body

관련 이야기 I also live with my family. There are 3 people in my family: my wife, my son, and me. My wife is really kind and good at cooking. My son is 4 years old. He is very active and likes playing baseball. We often go to mountains on the weekend.

질문 ① How many people are there in your family?

질문 ② Are you married? If so, do you have children?

질문 ③ What do you usually do with your family on the weekend?

Closing

마무리 Thank you for your kind answers.

가족과 함께 살고 있다고 하셨는데 괜찮으시다면 가족 관련 질문을 몇 가지 드리겠습니다. 저도 가족과 함께 삽니다. 제 가족은 아내, 아들 그리고 저까지 모두 셋입니다. 제 아내는 상냥하고 요리를 잘합니다. 아들은 4살입니다. 활동적인 아이고 야구를 좋아하죠. 우린 주말에 산에 자주 갑니다. 가족은 모두 몇 명입니까? 결혼하셨습니까? 그렇다면 자녀가 있습니까? 주말에는 가족과 보통 뭘 하십니까? 친절히 대답해 주셔서 감사합니다.

답변 tip!

직접 질문하는 롤플레이 유형은 주어진 상황에서 질문의 주제에 대해 3~4가지 관련 질문을 하는 것입니다. 제3자 또는 질문자 에바에게 질문하는 두 가지의 유형으로 나뉩니다. 직접질문하기는 주어진 상황에 대한 질문을 얼마나 적절하고 풍부하게 구성할 수 있는지가 중요합니다. 보다 효율적으로 대비하기 위해서는 주제별 (일상생활, 회사관련, 여가시간 등) 질문유형들에 익숙해지고 의문사활용을 통해 다양한 질문들을 만들어내는 연습을 하도록 합니다.

Q2. I often go to a park near my house. Please ask me 3 or 4 questions about the park I visit often.

내용구성하기	Introduction	☑ 인사말+질문 목적	
	Body	☑ 관련 이야기	☑ 질문 3가지
	Closing	☑ 마무리	

Introduction

인사말 +질문 목적 You said you often go to a park near your house. I'd like to ask some questions about the park you like to visit.

Body

관련 이야기 I also often go to a park in my neighborhood with my family. It takes only 10 minutes by foot. There is a big man-made lake in the middle. We often walk along the lake. Around the lake, we can see many trees and flowers. I like it because I can relax there and enjoy beautiful views.

질문 ① How far is the park from your house?

질문 ② What can you see at the park?

질문 ③ Why do you go there often?

Closing

마무리 Thank you for your kind answers.

집 근처 공원에 자주 간다고 하셨는데 즐겨 가는 공원에 대해 몇 가지 물어보겠습니다. 저도 가족과 동네 공원에 자주 갑니다. 걸어서 10분밖에 걸리지 않지요. 공원 한가운데는 큰 인공호수가 있습니다. 종종 호수 주변을 산책합니다. 호수 둘레에는 나무와 꽃들이 많이 있습니다. 그곳에서 쉬면서 아름다운 경치를 감상할 수 있어서 좋아합니다. 그 공원은 집에서 얼마나 먼가요? 공원에서는 뭘 볼 수 있나요? 왜 그곳에 자주 가나요? 친절히 대답해주셔서 감사합니다.

고득점 tip!

EVA 에게 질문하는 유형일 경우, 주제가 되는 Key word를 찾아내 그에 관련된 질문을 3~4개 하면 됩니다. 이 때, 단순히 질문만 하기보다 질문과 관련된 자신의 이야기를 적절하게 섞어서 답변하면 답변이 풍성해 질 수 있습니다.

 **Use the expressions in the Skill Up section to develop your sentences.**

- Introduction

- Body

- Closing

OPIc 도전! IM+

UNIT 16

전화로 질문하기

UNIT 16 전화로 질문하기

OPIc 도전! IM+

Learning Objectives

주어진 문제나 상황에 따라 문제 해결 및 정보 얻기 등의 특정 목적을 가지고 유선상으로 적절한 질문을 할 수 있다.

Frequently Asked Questions

- I'd like to give you a situation and ask you to act it out. You're planning to travel overseas with your friend. Call your friend and ask three or four questions about your trip.
- I'd like to give you a situation and ask you to act it out. You're going to take a trip and you have to rent a car. Call a rental agency and ask three or four questions about renting a car.
- I'd like to give you a situation and ask you to act it out. Let's say that a gym has just opened in your neighborhood. Call the gym and ask three or four questions about it.

Brainstorming

Step 1 Brainstorm key words and expressions about the topic.
Step 2 Use the words and expressions to brainstorm possible questions.

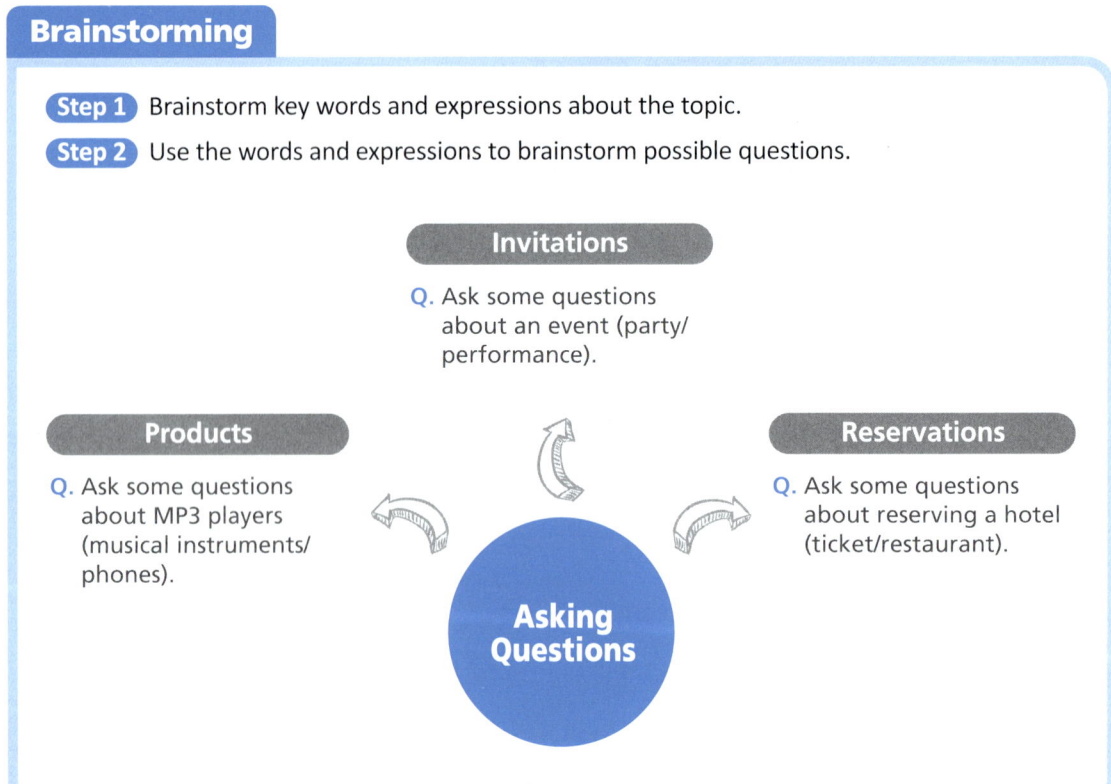

Invitations
Q. Ask some questions about an event (party/performance).

Products
Q. Ask some questions about MP3 players (musical instruments/phones).

Reservations
Q. Ask some questions about reserving a hotel (ticket/restaurant).

Asking Questions

Skill up! Expressions

여행관련 질문하기

Where do you want to go?
어디로 가고 싶은가요?

What kind of accommodations do you want to stay in?
어떤 종류의 숙박시설에 묵고 싶은가요?

How many days do you want to stay there?
그곳에서 얼마 동안 묵고 싶은가요?

Do you want to travel by plane or train?
비행기 또는 기차 중 어떤 수단을 이용하실 예정인가요?

랜트카 관련 질문하기

What kind of cars do you have available?
어떤 종류의 자동차들이 있습니까?

How much is it per day?
하루에 얼마입니까?

Are there any special discounts?
특별 할인 같은 게 있습니까?

Do you have a website where I can get more information?
자세한 정보가 나와있는 웹사이트가 있습니까?

헬스장 관련 질문하기

What kind of exercise equipment do you have?
어떤 종류의 운동 장비들이 있습니까?

How much is it for a month?
한 달에 얼마입니까?

Do you offer any special discounts?
특별 할인이 있습니까?

Do you have a website where I can get more information?
자세한 정보가 나와있는 웹사이트가 있습니까?

What time do you open and close?
영업시간은 어떻게 됩니까?

Useful Expressions

인사말
hello, this is

용건 말하기
I'm calling you about
I am wondering whether
this is concerning
I've got something to tell you about
there are some questions concerning
I'd like to ask

질문하기
first, I need to know if
is it possible to
finally, could you tell me
how can I

끝인사
thank you for your kind answer
I appreciate
you've been a big help

www.carrotenglish.com

How to Answer

Q1. I'd like to give you a situation and ask you to act it out. You're planning to travel with your friend. Call your friend and ask 3 or 4 questions about the trip.

내용구성하기		
	Introduction	☑ 인사말+전화 목적
	Body	☑ 질문 3가지
	Closing	☑ 끝인사

Introduction

인사말 +질문 목적 Hi, Jessica. This is Mike. I am calling you to talk about our trip.

Body

질문① 가고 싶은 곳 Where do you want to go this time? You know John went to Busan last weekend. He said it was really good. What do you think about going to Busan? I haven't been there yet. I found some information and there are many good hotels and guesthouses there.

질문② 숙박 시설 If we go to Busan, where do you want to stay? I'd prefer to stay in a hotel rather than a guesthouse.

질문③ 교통수단 We can get there by plane or train. It only takes 2 and a half hours by bullet train. Does that sound okay?

Closing

끝인사 Please let me know what you think. I'll call you back. Bye!

안녕 제시카, 나야, 마이크. 우리 여행에 대해 얘기 하려고 전화했어. 이번에 어디로 가고 싶어? 존이 지난 주에 부산에 갔었잖아. 정말 좋았대. 부산에 가는 거 어때? 나는 아직 부산에 안 가봤거든. 정보를 좀 찾아봤는데 괜찮은 호텔과 게스트하우스도 많이 있대. 만약 부산에 가게 되면 어디서 숙박하고 싶어? 난 게스트하우스보다는 호텔에서 숙박하는 편이 좋아. 부산에는 비행기나 기차로 갈 수 있어. 고속 열차로 2시간 반 밖에 안 걸리거든. 어때, 괜찮을 거 같아? 네 생각은 어떤지 알려줘. 다시 전화 걸게. 안녕!

답변 tip!

전화로 질문하기 유형은 상대방에게 직접 질문하는 것과 달리 전화통화하는 상황이 추가된 것입니다. 따라서 전화통화하는 상황에서 사용할 수 있는 표현들과 전화 대화형식(인사말→전화용건→질문하기→끝인사)을 익혀두는 것이 중요합니다. 각 주제별 출제될 수 있는 질문유형을 이해하고 전화를 받게 될 대상과 주제에 따라 전화 통화 형식의 답변을 준비하도록 합니다.

Q2. I'd like to give you a situation and ask you to act it out. You're going to travel and you have to rent a car. Call a rental agency and ask 3 or 4 questions about renting a car.

내용구성하기	Introduction	☑ 인사말+전화 목적		
	Body	☑ 관련 정보		☑ 질문 3가지
	Closing	☑ 끝인사		

Introduction
인사말 +질문 목적 Hello, I'd like to rent a car.

Body
관련 정보 I want to use it for 3 days starting next Monday. I need an automatic that seats 4 people.

질문① 렌트 가능한 차의 종류 What kinds of cars are available?

질문② 렌트 비용 And how much are they per day?

질문③ 웹사이트 여부 Do you have a website where I can get more information?

Closing
끝인사 My name is John and my phone number is 454-4545. Please call me back as soon as possible. Thank you.

여보세요, 차를 렌트하고 싶은데요. 다음주 월요일부터 3일간 사용하려고 합니다. 4인용 오토매틱 자동차가 필요합니다. 어떤 종류의 자동차들이 있습니까? 하루 렌트 가격은 얼마인가요? 좀더 자세한 정보를 얻을 수 있는 웹사이트가 있나요? 제 이름은 존이고 제 전화번호는 454-4545입니다. 가능한 빨리 전화해 주세요. 감사합니다.

고득점 tip!

바로 질문을 던지는 것 보다는 주어진 상황과 질문 하는 이유를 상세히 설명하는 것이 필요합니다. 상황 설명과 목적이 원활하게 연결되면 질문이 3개 이하가 되더라도 점수에 큰 영향을 끼치지 않습니다.

 **Use the expressions in the Skill Up section to develop your sentences.**

— Introduction

— Body

— Closing

OPIc
도전! IM+

UNIT 17

상황 설명하기

UNIT 17 상황 설명하기

OPIc 도전! IM+

Learning Objectives

문제나 상황 설명을 누가, 언제, 어디서, 무엇을, 어떻게, 왜 (5W1H)에 기반해 답변을 구성하여 듣는 이로 하여금 그 문제나 상황의 전말을 효과적으로 이해시킬 수 있는 답변을 할 수 있다.

주어진 상황을 직접 또는 전화로 설명해야 하는 질문 유형입니다. I'd like to give you a situation. 일단 상황을 설정해 줍니다. 또는 I'm sorry, but there is a problem you need to solve. 문제가 있다고 하네요. 설정을 잘 이해하고, Explain the situation. 상황 설명을 하라고 합니다.

Frequently Asked Questions

- I'd like to give you a situation and ask you to act it out. You're supposed to meet your friends this weekend. However, you cannot meet them for a certain reason. Call one of your friends and explain the situation.
- I'm sorry, but there is a problem you need to solve. You ordered food in a restaurant but you were served the wrong food. Explain the situation to a manager.
- I'm sorry, but you have a problem to solve. You made a reservation at a restaurant for dinner with your family. However, you find out your name is not on the online list of reservations. Explain the situation to the restaurant's manager.

Brainstorming

Step 1 Brainstorm key words and expressions about the topic.
Step 2 Use the words and expressions to brainstorm possible questions.

Appointments
Q. Explain why you cannot make it to a party (appointment/performance/flight).

Products
Q. Explain problems related to a phone (shoes/musical instrument).

Reservations
Q. Explain what is wrong with a hotel (restaurant/plane/movie ticket) you have booked.

Explanation

Skill up! Expressions

질문내용 설명하기

We were supposed to meet this weekend and I was looking forward to seeing you all.
이번 주말에 만나기로 한 약속에서 너희들을 모두 만나기를 고대하고 있었어.

I ordered the tuna sandwich.
전 참치 샌드위치를 주문했습니다.

I made a reservation for 4 people under the name of Justin for dinner.
저스틴이란 이름으로 저녁식사 4명을 예약했습니다.

문제점 설명하기

My boss just told me I have to go on a business trip this weekend.
방금 상사가 저보고 이번 주말에 출장을 가야 한다고 말해줬습니다.

I just found out I have to attend a very important business meeting this weekend.
이번 주말에 아주 중요한 비즈니스 회의에 참석해야 한다는 것을 방금 알았습니다.

I was just given a salmon sandwich as you can see, not the tuna sandwich.
보시다시피 연어 샌드위치가 나왔습니다. 참치 샌드위치가 아니고요.

I cannot find my name on the list of reservations on your website.
웹사이트 예약 명단에 제 이름이 나와 있지 않습니다.

마무리 의견 제시하기

I'm really sorry about canceling. I will join you next time for sure.
취소해서 정말 죄송합니다. 다음에는 꼭 참석하겠습니다.

Will I be able to get my tuna sandwich in the next 10 minutes?
10분 안에 참치 샌드위치를 받을 수 있을까요?

Please just cancel my order.
제 주문을 취소해주세요.

Can you get me a table for dinner?
디너용 자리를 마련해 주시겠어요?

Useful Expressions

전화 용건 및 문제상황 말하기
I am calling to
I have a problem to solve
there is a little problem with
I just found out that

직장에서 발생하는 상황
not working
out of order
e-mail never arrived
have an argument with my supervisor
miss the deadline
make a mistake

일상생활에서 발생하는 상황
notice a broken window
▶ call the building manager

scrape neighbor's car
▶ leave a note on his windshield

spill a can of paint
▶ have to clean it up

I was hoping we could
I have to
I wonder if you could

How to Answer

Q1. I'd like to give you a situation and ask you to act it out. You're supposed to meet your friends this weekend. However, you cannot meet them for a certain reason. Call one of your friends and explain the situation.

내용구성하기		
Introduction	☑ 인사+전화 목적	
Body	☑ 상황 설명	☑ 문제 상황
Closing	☑ 끝인사	

Introduction

인사말 +전화 목적 Hi, Jessica. This is Mike. I am calling you to talk about our plans this weekend.

Body

상황 설명 We were supposed to meet up and I was really looking forward to seeing all of you. But my boss asked me to go on a business trip to China at the last minute.

문제 상황 There are some serious issues with our Chinese branch. I couldn't say no. I am really sorry.

Closing

끝인사 Please let everyone know about the situation. I will come next time for sure. Sorry again. Bye.

여보세요 제시카, 나야, 마이크. 이번 주말 계획에 대해 얘기하려고 전화했어. 우리 다같이 만나기로 해서 정말 기대하고 있었는데, 사장님이 막판에 나보고 중국 출장을 가라고 했어. 중국 지사에 심각한 문제가 생겼거든. 안 된다고 말할 수가 없었어. 정말 미안해. 모두에게 상황 좀 설명해줘. 다음 번에는 꼭 갈게. 다시 한번 사과할게. 안녕.

답변 tip!

롤플레이의 한 유형으로써 질문에서 제시된 상황을 다른 대상에게 구체적으로 설명합니다. 질문에서 주어지는 문제상황을 정확히 파악하는 것이 중요합니다. 질문 유형으로는 일상생활 및 회사생활 등 다양한 상황에 대한 것이기 때문에 상황에 맞게 설명하는 연습이 필요합니다.

Q2. I'm sorry, but you have a problem to solve. You made a reservation at a restaurant for dinner with your family. However, you found out your name is not on the online list of reservations. Explain the situation to the restaurant's manager.

내용구성하기
- **Introduction** ☑ 인사+전화 목적
- **Body** ☑ 문제 상황   ☑ 상황 설명
- **Closing** ☑ 끝인사

Introduction
(인사말+전화 목적) Hello, this is Dan. I'd like to confirm my reservation with the manager.

Body
(문제 상황) I made a reservation for dinner 2 days ago, but I can't find my name on the reservation list.

(상황 설명) I made the reservation with someone named Susan. It's for my mother's birthday. Please check for whether there is anything wrong and let me know if you can give us a table for 4 people.

Closing
(끝인사) Please call me back. Thank you for your help.

여보세요, 댄이라고 합니다. 매니저와 저의 예약 내용을 확인하고 싶습니다. 이틀 전에 저녁식사를 예약했는데 예약 목록에서 제 이름을 찾을 수가 없습니다. 어머니 생신인 관계로 수잔이라는 분과 예약을 했었습니다.] 무엇이 잘못됐는지 확인해 주시고 4인용 테이블을 준비해 줄 수 있는지 알려 주십시오. 그럼 전화 주시기 바랍니다. 감사합니다.

주로 전화를 해서 상황을 설명하는 경우가 많지만 때때로 전화가 아닌 직접 해결해야 하는 경우도 있으니 주의 해서 답변하도록 합니다.

My Answer — Use the expressions in the Skill Up section to develop your sentences.

— Introduction

— Body

— Closing

OPIc 도전! IM+

UNIT 18
대안 제시하기

UNIT 18 대안 제시하기

OPIc 도전! IM+

Learning Objectives

주어진 문제나 상황의 전말을 본인의 말로 바꾸어 설명하고, 그에 대한 해결책 및 대안의 옵션을 2~3개 정도 제시 할 수 있다.

Frequently Asked Questions

- I'd like to give you a situation and ask you to act it out. You planned to go to the park with your friend this weekend. However, you found out the park is not open because it's under construction. Call your friend, explain the situation and give 3 or 4 alternatives.

- I'm sorry, but there is a problem you need to solve. Due to bad weather conditions, you have to cancel your plans to go to the beach with your friend. Call your friend and give your friend 3 or 4 suggestions.

- I'm sorry, but you have a problem to solve. You borrowed an MP3 player from your friend. However, you broke it. Call your friend to explain and give 2 or 3 suggestions.

Brainstorming

Step 1 Brainstorm key words and expressions about the topic.
Step 2 Use the words and expressions to brainstorm possible questions.

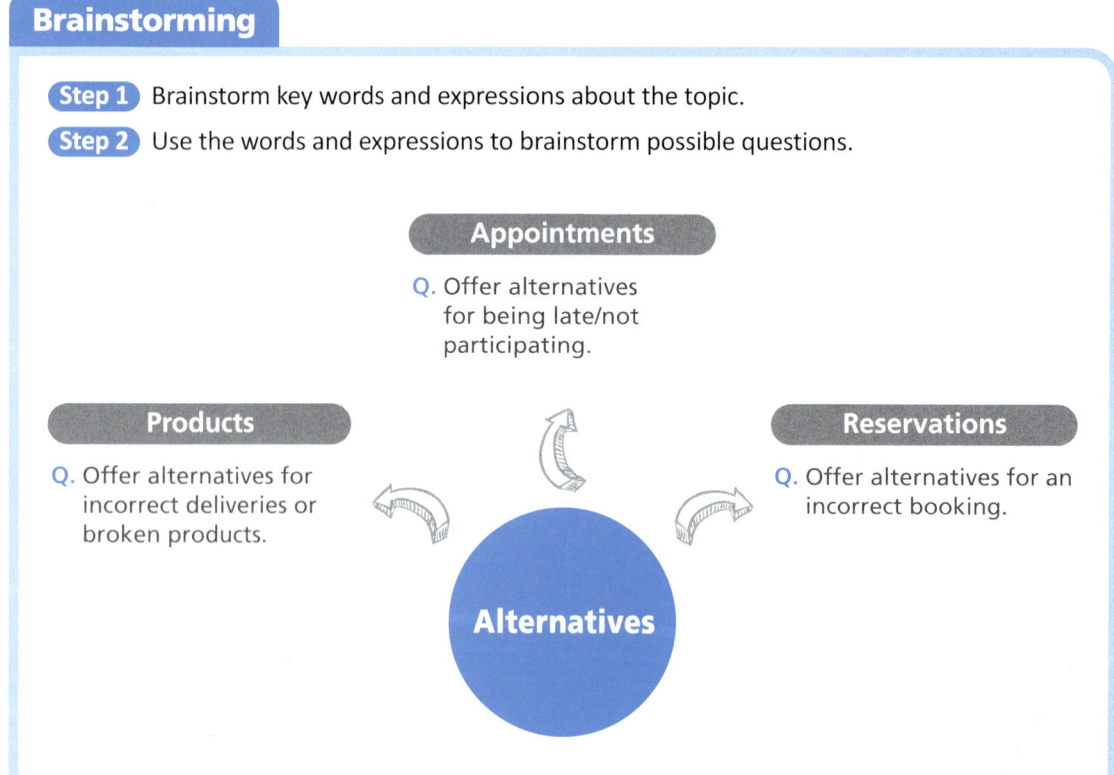

Skill up! Expressions

Useful Expressions

질문내용 설명하기

We made plans to go to the park this weekend.
우리는 이번 주말에 공원에 가기로 했었습니다.

We have plans to go to the beach.
우리는 해수욕장에 갈 계획입니다.

I borrowed your MP3 player.
내가 너한테 MP3 플레이어를 빌렸었잖아.

상황설명
it seems
it appears
it looks like

문제점 설명하기

I found out that the park is not open because it's under construction.
공원이 공사 중이라 문을 열지 않았다는 것을 알았습니다.

I checked the weather forecast and it said it will rain tomorrow.
날씨 예보를 확인해보니 내일 비가 온다고 합니다.

I dropped it accidently.
실수로 떨어뜨렸어.

문제 상황
set another day
proceed as planned
change direction
set a meeting agenda now or
wait until next week
have themeeting now

have something urgent come up
have some news
have a problem arise

제안 주기

Let's see a movie and go shopping instead.
대신에 영화를 보고 쇼핑을 갑시다.

How about going to a pub in town?
동네 펍에 가는 건 어떨까요?

What do think about going to the swimming pool near your house?
너희 집 근처에 있는 수영장에 가는 건 어떻게 생각해?

I want to buy you a new one.
새로운 것으로 사줄게.

I can take it to a repair shop.
수리점에 맡길게.

If you want, I will buy you some clothes instead.
원한다면 대신 옷을 사줄게.

대안제시
let's think about
what do you think of
what about
do you think we could/should
what if we
would it be possible to
what are our options
can we

some options
some ideas
better solutions

How to Answer

Q1. I'm sorry, but there is a problem you need to solve. Due to bad weather conditions, you have to cancel your plans to go to the beach with your friend. Call your friend and give your friend 3 or 4 suggestions.

내용구성하기		
Introduction	☑ 인사말+전화 목적	
Body	☑ 상황 설명 ☑ 문제 상황 ☑ 대안 제시	
Closing	☑ 끝인사	

Introduction

인사말 +전화 목적 Hi, Jessica. This is Mike. I am calling you to talk about our weekend plans.

Body

상황 설명 We were supposed to go to the beach this weekend and I was really looking forward to it.

문제 상황 But I just checked the weather forecast and it said it will rain this weekend. I think we should go another time. Let's do something else this weekend.

대안 제시① How about watching a movie? Or going shopping at the mall near your house?

대안 제시② If you want to go swimming, we can go to the indoor swimming pool.

Closing

끝인사 Please let me know what you think. I'll be waiting for your call. Bye.

안녕 제시카, 나야, 마이크. 우리 주말 계획에 대해 얘기하려고 전화했어. 우리 이번 주말에 해수욕장에 가기로 했었잖아, 정말 기대 중이었는데 말이야. 방금 날씨 예보를 확인해 보니까 주말에 비가 올 거래. 다음에 가야 할 것 같아. 이번 주말에는 다른 것을 하자. 영화를 보는 건 어때? 아니면 너희 집 근처 쇼핑몰에서 쇼핑하는 건? 수영하러 가고 싶으면 실내 수영장에 갈 수도 있어. 네 생각은 어떤지 말해줘. 전화 기다릴게, 안녕.

답변 tip!

롤플레이 유형 중 가장 난이도가 높은 질문입니다. 질문에서 제시된 문제상황 설명과 대안을 함께 제시해야 합니다. 따라서 상황 설명보다는 대안제시에 비중을 두고 자신의 입장에서 대안을 제시하도록 합니다. 일상생활 및 회사생활 관련하여 다양한 상황이 제시됩니다.

Q2. I'm sorry, but you have a problem to solve. You borrowed an MP3 player from your friend. However, you broke it. Call your friend to explain and give 2 or 3 alternatives.

내용구성하기

Introduction	☑ 인사말+전화 목적	
Body	☑ 상황 설명	☑ 대안 제시
Closing	☑ 끝인사	

Introduction

인사말+전화 목적 Hello, this is Dan. I am really sorry. I broke the MP3 player that I borrowed from you last week.

Body

상황 설명 This morning I dropped it accidently. I called the company and they said it can be fixed. They gave me directions to a repair shop as well.

대안 제시① If you don't mind, I will take it there and get it fixed.

대안 제시②,③ But if you don't like that idea, I am willing to buy you a new one or give you some money as compensation. It's all my fault and I am really sorry once again.

Closing

끝인사 Please call me back. Don't hesitate to tell me what you want me to do. I will wait for your call. Bye.

안녕, 댄이야. 정말 미안해. 지난주에 너한테 빌린 MP3플레이어가 고장 났어. 오늘 아침에 실수로 떨어뜨렸거든. 회사에 연락했는데 고칠 수 있대. 수리점 위치도 알려줬어. 괜찮으면 내가 수리점에 갖고 가서 고쳐 올게. 하지만 그게 싫으면 내가 새로운 것으로 사줄게. 아니면 돈으로 보상해 줄게. 이건 모두 내 잘못이야, 다시 한번 정말 미안해. 전화해줘. 주저하지 말고 네가 하고 싶은 대로 나한테 알려줘. 그럼 전화 기다릴게. 안녕.

고득점 tip!

주어진 상황을 직접 또는 전화로 설명하고 대안을 제시해야 하는 질문 유형이니 여러가지 상황에서 사용 가능한 제안들을 미리 익혀 두는 것이 좋습니다. 대안 제시도 중요하지만 주어진 문제 상황을 자세하게 설명하는 것에 더욱 신경을 써야 합니다.

 **Use the expressions in the Skill Up section to develop your sentences.**

— Introduction

— Body

— Closing

II

실력다지기

☑ **Part 4 돌발주제**

Unit 19 | 집안일
Unit 20 | 외식
Unit 21 | 재활용
Unit 22 | 계절
Unit 23 | 약속
Unit 24 | 쇼핑

OPIc
도전!
IM+

OPIc
도전! IM+

UNIT **19**

집안일

UNIT 19 집안일

OPIc 도전! IM+

Learning Objectives

집에서 하는 일거리를 소개하고 어린 시절 기억에 남는 집안일 등에 대해 이야기 할 수 있다.

Frequently Asked Questions

- What housework do you usually do at home? What are your responsibilities at home?
- Tell me about your favorite and least favorite household chores.
- What kind of housework did you do when you were young? Tell me how you helped out around the house in your childhood.

Brainstorming

Step 1 Brainstorm key words and expressions about the topic.
Step 2 Use the words and expressions to brainstorm possible questions.

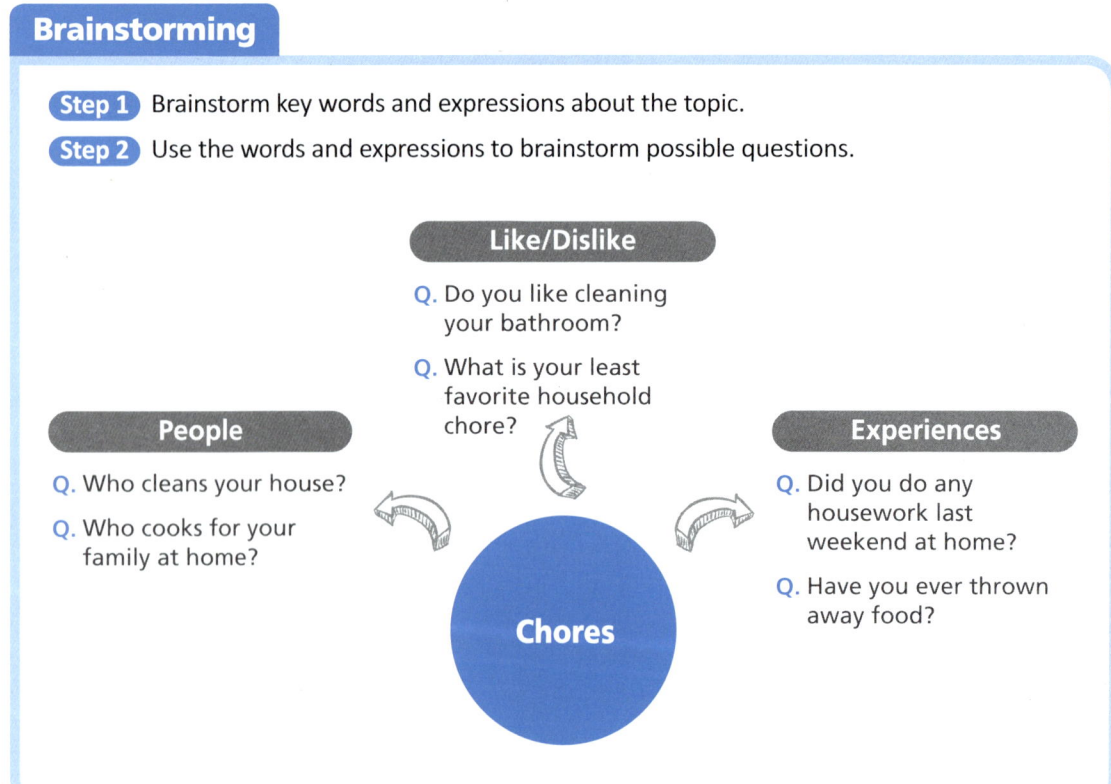

Skill up! Expressions

집안일
I vacuum the house. / I clean the bathroom.
집을 청소합니다. / 욕실을 청소합니다.

I wash the dishes. / I do the laundry.
설거지를 합니다. / 빨래를 합니다.

I set the table. / I fold the laundry.
밥상을 차립니다. / 빨래를 갭니다.

I go grocery shopping. / I throw away the food scraps.
장을 봅니다. / 음식물 쓰레기를 버립니다.

집안일 관련 표현
I feel refreshed after finishing all my housework.
집안일을 모두 끝내면 기분 전환이 됩니다.

It takes a long time to finish.
마치려면 시간이 오래 걸립니다.

It's dirty and stinky.
더럽고 냄새나죠.

It's troublesome.
번거로워요.

I hate it but my wife always asks me to do it.
전 싫어하지만 항상 아내가 저보고 해달라고 합니다.

I feel rewarded after finishing.
끝내고 나면 보람을 느낍니다.

어린 시절 집안일
I organized my books and toys when I was young.
어렸을 때는 책과 장난감을 정리했습니다.

I had to take care of my little sister.
여동생을 돌봐야 했습니다.

I often ran errands for my mother.
엄마가 시킨 심부름을 종종 했습니다.

Useful Expressions

집안일
scrub the bathtub
dust my bookshelves
sweep my backyard
wipe dirty surfaces
clean the window

집안일 관련 감정 표현
achieved | pound | pleasant | cheerful | delightful | exhilarated | boastful

집안일 관련 느낌
smelly | unpleasant | difficult | damp | musty | irritating | unwanted

no one else will do it
it is my responsibility
I have to do it
I need to educate my kids

How to Answer

Q1. What housework do you usually do at home? What are your responsibilities at home?

내용구성하기		
Introduction	☑ 집안일 소개	
Body	☑ 내가 하는 집안일 3가지	☑ 다른 사람이 하는 집안일
Closing	☑ 느낌 및 의견	

Introduction

집안일 소개 I'll tell you about what I usually do at home. We are a double income household, so I share the housework with my wife.

Body

내가 하는 집안일 ① First of all, I clean our bedroom. After organizing our things, I vacuum the floors.

내가 하는 집안일 ② Secondly, I do the laundry. It's easy to do, but I hate hanging out the washing.

내가 하는 집안일 ③ Lastly, I'm responsible for taking care of the dog. I feed it and take it for a walk every day.

남편이 하는 집안일 My wife does other things, such as cleaning the bathrooms and taking out the trash and recycling.

Closing

느낌 및 의견 I don't enjoy doing housework, but I feel good after it is all done.

집에서 보통 하는 일에 대해 얘기해보겠습니다. 우리는 맞벌이 가족입니다. 그래서 아내와 집안일을 분담합니다. 먼저 침실을 청소합니다. 물건 정리를 마치면 청소기로 바닥을 청소합니다. 두번째로 빨래를 합니다. 하기 쉬운 일이지만 빨래를 너는 건 싫어합니다. 마지막으로 개를 돌보는 건 제 책임입니다. 밥을 주고 매일 산책을 데리고 갑니다. 아내와 나머지 일들을 합니다. 화장실 청소나, 쓰레기 버리기, 재활용하기 같은 거죠. 전 집안일 하는 것을 좋아하지 않지만, 모두 마치고 나면 기분이 좋아집니다.

답변 tip!

집안일은 최근들어 돌발로 자주 출제되는 문제유형 입니다. 집안일과 관련된 다양한 표현과 질문유형에 익숙해 지고 답변을 연습하도록 합니다.

Q2. Tell me about your favorite and least favorite household chores.

내용구성하기	Introduction	☑ 내가 하는 집안일 소개		
	Body	☑ 좋아하는 집안일	☑ 싫어하는 집안일	☑ 이유
	Closing	☑ 느낌 및 의견		

Introduction

내가 하는 집안일 소개 I do chores at home like washing the dishes, vacuuming, and doing the laundry.

Body

좋아하는 집안일 & 이유 My favorite chore is folding the laundry. When the washing is dry, I fold everything. It's easy and fun to do. When it is folded neatly, I feel satisfied.

싫어하는 집안일 & 이유 On the other hand, my least favorite chore is cooking. I'm not good at it and find it really difficult, so I prefer eating out to cooking at home. Once in a while my husband cooks for me. I think he is a much better cook than me, because he can make many kinds of Korean food and some Italian dishes as well.

Closing

느낌 및 의견 Those are my favorite and least favorite household chores.

집에서 설거지, 청소기 밀기, 빨래와 같은 일들을 합니다. 가장 좋아하는 집안일은 빨래 개기입니다. 널은 빨래들이 마르면 모두 갭니다. 쉽고 재밌습니다. 잘 개어 놓은 빨래를 보면 만족스럽습니다. 반대로 제가 가장 싫어하는 집안일은 요리입니다. 요리를 잘 하지 못하고 힘들어서, 전 집에서 요리하는 것보다 외식을 선호합니다. 어쩌다 가끔 남편이 요리를 해주기도 합니다. 저보다 훨씬 더 요리를 잘하죠. 남편은 여러 가지 한식은 물론 몇 개의 이탈리아 음식도 할 줄 압니다. 이런 것들이 제가 가장 좋아하고, 가장 싫어하는 집안일입니다.

고득점 tip!

집안일을 할 때 어떤 순서로 하는지 순차적으로 이야기 하거나 좋아하는 집안일과 싫어하는 집안일을 비교하여 구체적인 이유를 든다면 풍성한 답변이 될 수 있습니다.

 **My Answer** — Use the expressions in the Skill Up section to develop your sentences.

− Introduction

− Body

− Closing

OPIc
도전! IM+

UNIT 20

외식

UNIT 20 외식

OPIc 도전! IM+

Learning Objectives

좋아하는 식당의 및 음식에 대해 소개하고 외식 경험에 대해 이야기 할 수 있다.

Frequently Asked Questions

- How often do you eat out? When you eat out, who do you usually go with?
- Tell me about a restaurant you ate at recently. Where did you go? What did you eat?
- Please tell me about your favorite restaurant. What kind of food do they serve? What makes it better than other restaurants?

Brainstorming

Step 1 Brainstorm key words and expressions about the topic.
Step 2 Use the words and expressions to brainstorm possible questions.

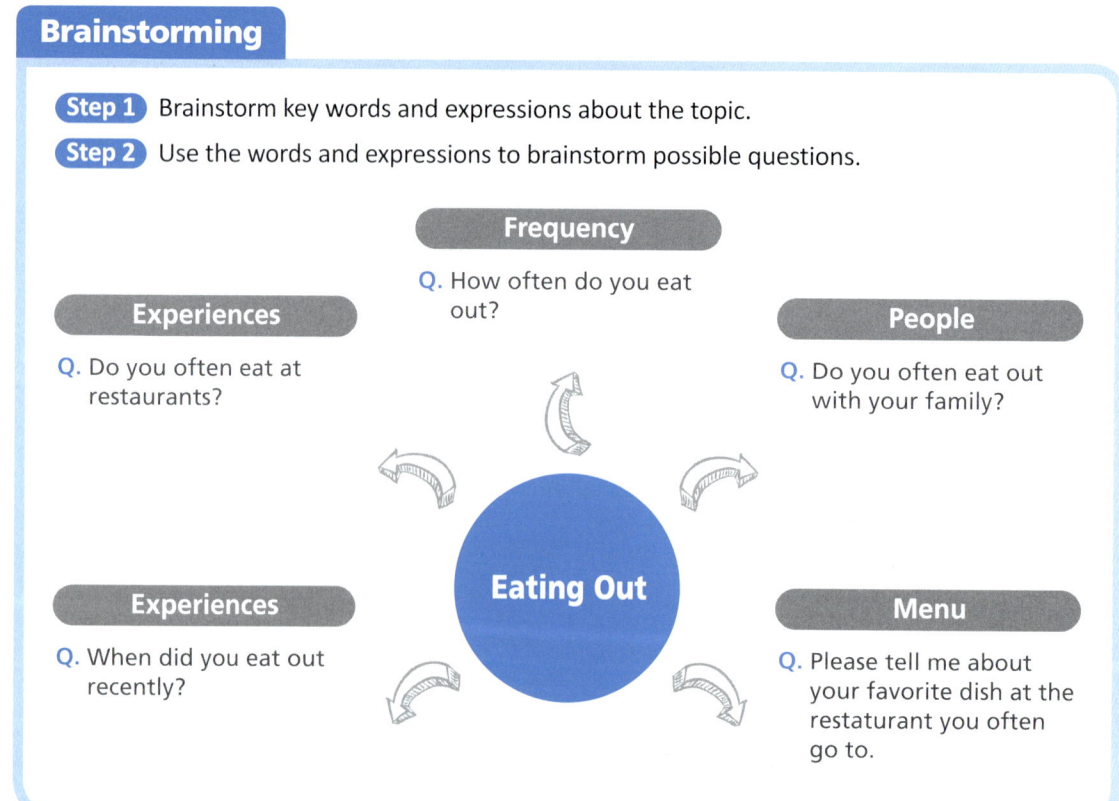

Skill up! Expressions

좋아하는 식당 및 음식

I often go to a **Korean restaurant** called Malipo.
저는 말리포라는 한식당에 자주 갑니다.

I like a Chinese restaurant named Pal Sunsaeng in my neighborhood.
동네에 있는 팔선당이라는 중식당을 좋아합니다.

They **serve** many kinds of Chinese food.
여러 가지 중국요리가 나옵니다.

My favorite restaurant is Little India, an Indian restaurant near my office.
가장 좋아하는 레스토랑은 리틀 인디아라는 사무실 근처의 인도식당입니다.

I love their **pasta**.
전 그곳의 파스타를 좋아합니다.

My favorite food there is Samgyetang.
제일 좋아하는 음식은 삼계탕입니다.

외식 경험 말하기

I went to an Italian restaurant **for my sister's birthday** last week.
지난 주 여동생 생일에 이탈리아 식당에 갔습니다.

I **ate out** at a buffet with my family 2 days ago.
이틀 전 가족과 뷔페에서 외식을 했습니다.

My girlfriend and I went to a barbeque restaurant in Suwon on the weekend.
주말에는 여자친구와 함께 수원에 있는 바베큐 식당에 갔습니다.

식당의 장점

They serve the **best steak in town**.
동네 최고의 스테이크가 있습니다.

The food there is always **fresh and delicious**.
음식이 항상 신선하고 맛있습니다.

I often go there because of **the reasonable prices and friendly staff**.
가격이 합리적이고 직원이 친절해서 자주 갑니다.

Useful Expressions

좋아하는 식당
Japanese restaurant
Thai restaurant
American restaurant
Vietnamese restaurant
steak house
family restaurant
noodle house
buffet

have | carry

음식
spicy soup
appetizer
fish dishes
seafood dishes
calamari fries
dressing
drinks
risotto
meatballs
sushi
sashimi
teriyaki chicken

외식경험
for my friend's wedding
for the meeting
after the conference
before going to a movie
for having a party
to entertain a customer

dine out
go out

식당의 장점
the most delicious pasta
the freshest seafood
the most beautiful desert

clean and neat
sweet and savory

its convenient parking lot
its great location
good atmosphere
delicious dishes

How to Answer

Q1. Please tell me about your favorite restaurant. What kind of food do they serve?

내용구성하기		
	Introduction	☑ 좋아하는 식당 소개
	Body	☑ 그 식당을 좋아하는 이유 3가지
	Closing	☑ 느낌 및 의견

Introduction

좋아하는 식당 소개 I like eating out. I know many good restaurants near my house and office. My favorite food is sushi and one of my favorite restaurants for it is a Japanese restaurant called Jun Sushi.

Body

그 식당을 좋아하는 이유① 음식 I love to go there to enjoy nice sushi. They always use fresh ingredients.

그 식당을 좋아하는 이유② 분위기&서비스 Also, I like its atmosphere and friendly staff. They play quiet Japanese music there and it's filled with Japanese dolls and decorations.

그 식당을 좋아하는 이유③ 가격 Moreover, it's relatively cheap, so I often take my other friends there.

Closing

느낌 및 의견 I like Jun Sushi very much. If you like Japanese food, it's a place I highly recommend trying.

전 외식을 좋아합니다. 집 근처와 회사 근처에 좋은 레스토랑을 많이 알고 있습니다. 가장 좋아하는 음식은 초밥이고 제일 좋아하는 초밥집은 준 스시라는 일식당입니다. 그곳으로 맛있는 초밥을 먹으러 가는 것을 좋아합니다. 그 초밥집은 항상 신선한 재료를 사용하죠. 또한 그곳의 분위기와 친절한 직원들도 맘에 듭니다. 조용한 일본 음악이 흐르고 일본식 인형, 장식품들로 꾸며져 있습니다. 게다가 상대적으로 가격도 저렴합니다. 그래서 종종 친구들을 데리고 갑니다. 준 스시는 제가 정말 좋아하는 곳입니다. 혹시 일본 음식을 좋아하신다면 꼭 한번 방문하시길 추천합니다.

답변 tip!

외식하기 에서는 주로 자주 가는 식당 묘사, 좋아하는 메뉴, 최근 외식한 경험 등의 문제가 출제되니 관련 표현들을 익혀 예상질문에 대한 답변을 미리 준비하도록 합니다.

Q2. Tell me about a restaurant you ate at recently. Where did you go? What did you eat?

내용구성하기

Introduction ☑ 최근 외식 경험
Body ☑ 외식을 한 이유 ☑ 음식의 맛
Closing ☑ 느낌 및 의견

Introduction

최근 외식 경험 I will tell you about a restaurant I ate out at recently. Last Sunday, I went to a Japanese restaurant with my wife.

Body

외식을 한 이유 Actually, it was a conveyor-belt sushi restaurant. During the week, I usually eat 3 meals a day at my company cafeteria. That's why I like eating out on the weekend with my friends or family for a change.

음식의 맛 I enjoyed various kinds of sushi like salmon and tuna for dinner there. The food was delicious and fresh.

Closing

느낌 및 의견 I think I will become a regular there.

최근에 다녀온 식당에 대해 얘기해보겠습니다. 지난 일요일 아내와 함께 일본식 레스토랑에 갔다 왔습니다. 회전 초밥집이었는데요, 전 주중에 하루 세끼를 회사 식당에서 먹습니다. 그래서 주말에는 기분 전환으로 친구나 가족과 함께 외식하는 것을 좋아합니다. 저녁으로 연어나 참치 초밥 같은 다양한 초밥들을 먹었습니다. 음식도 맛있었고 신선했습니다. 그곳의 단골이 될 것 같습니다.

고득점 tip!

좋아하는 식당에서 정말 맛있게 먹었던 음식과 왜 그 음식을 좋아하는지 또는 식당의 인테리어는 어떻고, 다른 식당들과의 차이점은 무엇인지 등을 구체적으로 제시한다면 답변이 풍부해 질 수 있습니다. 외식 경험에 대해 답할 때는 과거시제를 사용하는 것에 주의하세요.

My Answer — Use the expressions in the Skill Up section to develop your sentences.

- Introduction

- Body

- Closing

OPIc
도전! IM+

UNIT **21**

재활용

UNIT 21 재활용

OPIc 도전! IM+

Learning Objectives

평소 재활용 활동에 대해 소개하고 한국의 재활용 하는 방법에 대해 이야기 할 수 있다.

Frequently Asked Questions

- Tell me about recycling in your country.
- How do you recycle at home? How often do you recycle?
- Tell me about an unforgettable experience you had while recycling.
- Describe each step of recycling from the beginning to the end.

Brainstorming

Step 1 Brainstorm key words and expressions about the topic.
Step 2 Use the words and expressions to brainstorm possible questions.

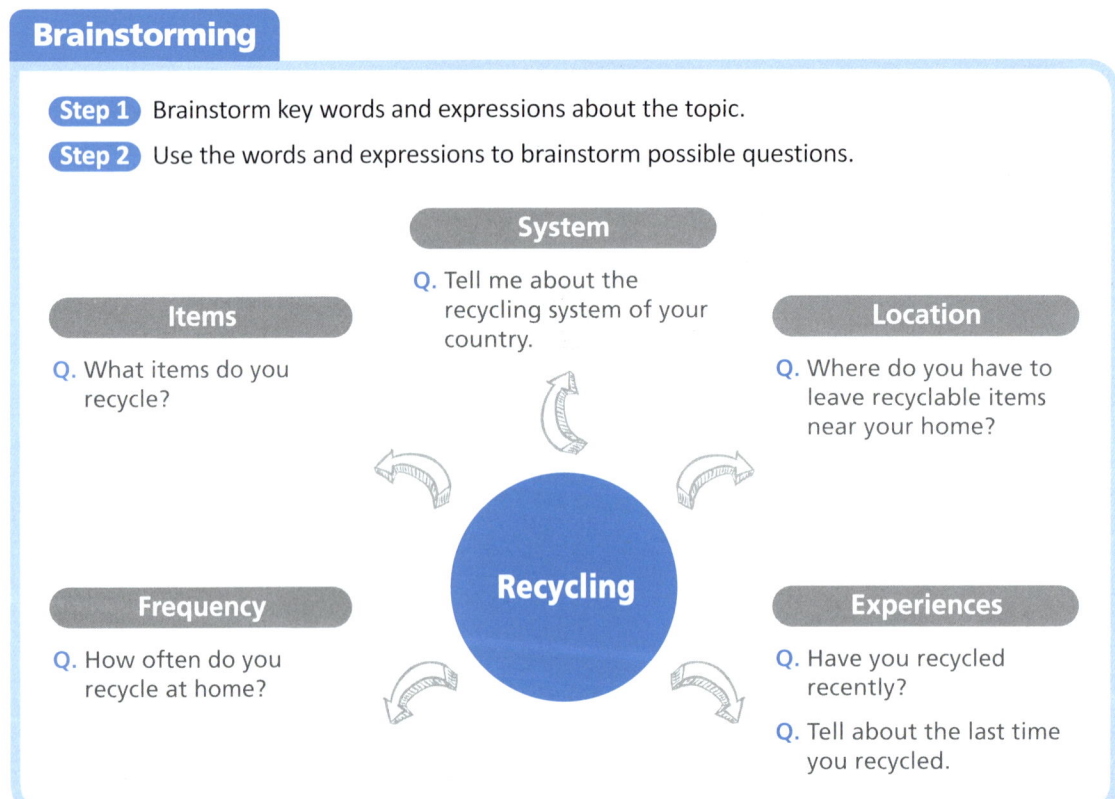

System
Q. Tell me about the recycling system of your country.

Items
Q. What items do you recycle?

Location
Q. Where do you have to leave recyclable items near your home?

Frequency
Q. How often do you recycle at home?

Recycling

Experiences
Q. Have you recycled recently?
Q. Tell about the last time you recycled.

Skill up! Expressions

한국의 재활용

There are very **strict rules** about recycling in Korea.
한국은 재활용 관련 규제가 매우 엄격합니다.

The recycling system in Korea is very **effective and strict**.
한국의 재활용 시스템은 효율적이고 엄격합니다.

Regular waste has to be bagged in a special bag, which you have to buy from a store.
일반 쓰레기는 특별한 봉투에 담아야 하는데, 이 봉투는 상점에서 구입해야 합니다.

Recyclable items are picked up for free.
재활용이 가능한 품목은 무료로 수거해 갑니다.

People have to recycle items that are made of paper, plastic, glass, and metal.
종이, 플라스틱, 유리, 금속으로 된 물품들은 재활용 해야 합니다.

Recycling is **important** for the environment.
재활용은 환경에 중요합니다.

재활용 하기

I **separate different recyclable items** like metal cans and plastic containers.
금속 캔과 플라스틱 상자 같은 재활용 품목들을 따로 분리합니다.

There are designated areas to **put recyclable items**.
재활용 품목을 넣도록 정해진 구역이 있습니다.

I **take them to the pickup area** once a week.
일주일에 한번 수거 구역에 재활용품을 갖다 둡니다.

Every Thursday, a truck comes and picks up the recyclable items.
매주 목요일 트럭이 와서 재활용품목들을 수거해 갑니다.

Recycling is a bit **troublesome**.
재활용은 약간 번거롭습니다.

Useful Expressions

한국의 재활용
well-implemented | well-planned | meticulous | detailed | efficient | controlling

중요성
meaningful | necessary | essential | crucial | vital | significant | required | needed

재활용 하기
rinse recyclable items
identify recyclable item like paper and plastic
group them into 4 categories
collect recyclable items
keep recyclable waste
throw them away
throw them out
dump them

빈도
on Thursdays
every second Friday
every 1st and 15th

느낌
challenging | difficult | bothersome | upsetting | annoying

How to Answer

Q1. Tell me about recycling in your country.

내용구성하기	Introduction	☑ 한국의 재활용		
	Body	☑ 재활용 품목	☑ 재활용 빈도	☑ 일반쓰레기 처리 방법
	Closing	☑ 느낌 및 의견		

Introduction

한국의 재활용 Recycling in Korea is pretty effective and strict.

Body

재활용 품목 People have to recycle items made of paper, plastic, glass, and metal. Recyclable items are picked up for free. It encourages people to recycle.

재활용 빈도 Once a week, the recyclable items are picked up.

일반 쓰레기 처리 방법 On the other hand, regular waste has to be bagged in a special bag, which you have to buy from a store. Also, you have to buy a separate bag to dispose of food waste.

Closing

느낌 및 의견 Honestly, the recycling policy is strict and following it is troublesome. However, it's really important for the environment.

한국의 재활용 제도는 아주 효율적이고 엄격합니다. 종이, 플라스틱, 유리, 금속으로 된 품목은 재활용해야 합니다. 재활용품은 무료로 수거됩니다. 사람들이 재활용을 하게 권장합니다. 일주일에 한번 재활용품이 수거됩니다. 반대로 일반 쓰레기는 특별 봉투에 담아야 하는데 이 봉투는 상점에서 구입해야 합니다. 또한 음식물 쓰레기를 버릴 별도의 봉투도 구입해야 합니다. 재활용 정책은 엄격하고 솔직히 규칙을 지키는 일은 조금 번거롭습니다. 하지만 환경에 정말 중요한 일이지요.

답변 tip!

재활용하기 질문 유형으로 일반적인 문제들 뿐만 아니라 롤플레잉 문제들의 출제 가능성도 염두 하여 학습해야 합니다. 전반적인 재활용 시스템이나 절차 등의 사전 지식을 미리 숙지하여 대답할 때 망설임 없이 시작할 수 있도록 합니다.

Q2. How do you recycle at home? How often do you recycle?

내용구성하기	Introduction	☑ 집에서의 재활용
	Body	☑ 재활용 절차
	Closing	☑ 느낌 및 의견

Introduction

집에서의 재활용 I will tell you about how I recycle at home. I live in an apartment building. There are very strict rules about recycling.

Body

재활용 절차① First, I separate the different types of recyclable items like plastic bottles, metal cans, and newspapers and I put them in different bags.

재활용 절차② Every Monday, I take the bags out to the recycling area next to my apartment building. There are different containers for each recyclable item, so I have to put the items into the correct container.

Closing

느낌 및 의견 Frankly speaking, recycling is a bit troublesome. But, I know it's really necessary for the environment, so I'm happy to do it.

집에서 재활용하는 방법에 대해 얘기해보겠습니다. 저는 아파트에 살고 있습니다. 이곳의 재활용 관련 규칙은 매우 엄격합니다. 먼저 플라스틱 병, 금속 캔, 신문 같은 여러 가지 재활용 품목을 분리한 후 각기 다른 봉투에 넣습니다. 월요일마다 아파트 건물 옆에 있는 재활용 구역에 그 봉투를 버립니다. 재활용 품목마다 정해진 각각의 통이 있기 때문에 각 통에 해당되는 재활용품을 넣어야 합니다. 솔직히 말하면 재활용은 조금 번거롭습니다. 하지만 환경에 필수적인 일이란 것을 알기 때문에 기꺼이 실천하고 있습니다.

혼동하기 쉬운 단어 사용에 유의하면서 연습해 봅시다.

Recycle 재활용하다   Recycling 재활용   Recyclable 재활용 가능한

 **Use the expressions in the Skill Up section to develop your sentences.**

— Introduction

— Body

— Closing

OPIc
도전! IM+

UNIT 22

계절

UNIT 22 계절

OPIc 도전! IM+

Learning Objectives

한국의 사계절에 대해 소개하고 계절별 특징 및 활동 등에 대해 이야기 할 수 있다.

Frequently Asked Questions

- Tell me about the seasons in your country. How's the weather in each season?
- What's your favorite season? What activities do you do in that season?
- What activities do people usually do in your country in each season? What are the most popular activities for each season?

Brainstorming

Step 1 Brainstorm key words and expressions about the topic.
Step 2 Use the words and expressions to brainstorm possible questions.

Experiences
Q. Do you have any memorable experiences that happened in summer/winter?

Weather
Q. How's the weather in summer and winter in your country?
Q. Does it rain often in the summer in your country?

Activities
Q. Whar are the most popular activities for each season?
Q. What activities do you enjoy in summer/winter?

Seasons

Skill up! Expressions

한국의 계절

There are four **distinct** seasons in Korea: spring, summer, fall, and winter.
한국은 봄, 여름, 가을, 겨울의 사계절이 뚜렷합니다.

The **weather is very nice** and **mild in spring and fall**.
봄과 가을의 날씨는 아주 좋고 온화합니다.

It's perfect picnic weather.
소풍에 완벽한 날씨입니다.

It is **extremely hot in summer**. We also have the **rainy season during summer**.
여름에는 굉장히 덥습니다. 여름에는 장마철도 있습니다.

It's very **hot and humid in summer**.
여름철은 아주 덥고 습합니다.

It's **freezing cold** and it **sometimes snows in winter**.
겨울은 굉장히 춥고 종종 눈이 내립니다.

계절별 활동

It's nice to **enjoy outdoor activities** because of the nice, warm weather.
따뜻하고 좋은 날씨 때문에 야외 활동을 즐기기에 좋습니다.

I often **go on picnics** with my family in spring.
봄에는 종종 가족과 함께 나들이를 갑니다.

I **go hiking** to see beautiful autumn leaves in autumn.
가을철의 아름다운 단풍을 보기 위해 하이킹을 갑니다.

Many people in Korea **go to beach** and **enjoy water sports**.
많은 한국 사람들이 해수욕장에 가서 물놀이를 즐깁니다.

I often **go to ski resorts** during winter.
겨울에는 스키장에 자주 갑니다.

Useful Expressions

한국의 사계절
clear
distinctive

계절풍경 묘사
covered in lush green
wrapped in many colors
alive with new growth
lose their leaves in fall
start to sprout in spring
turn lush and green in summer

계절별 날씨 및 특징
summer | the rainy season
spring | the planting season
winter | the cold season
winter | dry, cold, and freezing
fall | pleasant and cool
fall | nice and mild
fall | turn chilly

계절활동
celebrate a harvest festival in fall
participate in summer vacation events
going skiing in winter
going hiking in fall
gardening in spring

계절음식
local produce
fresh-picked vegetables
domestic fruit

How to Answer

Q1. Tell me about the seasons in your country. How's the weather in each season?

내용구성하기		
	Introduction	☑ 우리나라 계절 소개
	Body	☑ 계절별 특징
	Closing	☑ 느낌 및 의견

Introduction

우리나라 계절 소개 As I mentioned, I live in Korea. It has 4 distinct seasons: spring, summer, fall, and winter.

Body

봄&가을 소개 The weather is usually nice and warm in the spring and fall. It's mild and perfect to go on a picnic. But these days because of yellow dust, sometimes we can't enjoy outdoor activities in spring.

여름 소개 On the other hand, the summer is very hot in Korea. It rains often and it's very hot and humid. Many people enjoy water sports in this season.

겨울 소개 Finally, winter is the polar opposite. It's freezing cold and it sometimes snows.

Closing

느낌 및 의견 I think we are lucky because we can enjoy different scenery and activities each season in my country.

말씀 드렸듯이 저는 한국에 삽니다. 한국은 봄, 여름, 가을, 겨울 사계절이 뚜렷합니다. 봄과 가을의 날씨는 따뜻하고 좋습니다. 온화해서 나들이 가기에 완벽합니다. 하지만 요새는 황사 때문에 봄철에도 야외활동을 즐기지 못하는 경우가 종종 있습니다. 반면 한국의 여름은 매우 덥습니다. 비도 자주 오고 날씨도 덥고 습합니다. 이 계절에는 많은 이들이 물놀이를 즐깁니다. 마지막으로 겨울은 완전히 반대입니다. 굉장히 춥고 가끔 눈이 내립니다. 한국에서는 매 계절마다 다양한 경치와 활동을 즐길 수 있어서 다행이라고 생각합니다.

답변 tip!

돌발 질문으로 자주 등장하는 주제 중 하나가 계절에 관한 것입니다. 자주 출제되는 질문의 유형으로는 1) 계절활동, 2) 좋아하는 계절, 3) 계절(날씨) 변화 및 묘사 등에 관련된 것입니다. 계절에 대한 어휘 및 표현들을 익혀 미리 연습해보도록 합니다.

Q2. What's your favorite season? What activities do you do in that season?

내용구성하기
- **Introduction** ☑ 가장 좋아하는 계절
- **Body** ☑ 좋아하는 계절 ☑ 하는 활동
- **Closing** ☑ 느낌 및 의견

Introduction

가장 좋아하는 계절 There are four distinct seasons in Korea: spring, summer, fall, and winter. Out of all the seasons, my favorite one is fall.

Body

좋아하는 계절에 하는 활동 ① The weather is very nice and the temperatures are very mild in the fall, so it's good for activities like going to the park or playing badminton. I often do outdoor activities with my wife during the week.

좋아하는 계절에 하는 활동 ② Also, the fall scenery is very beautiful. In fall, trees' leaves change from green to yellow or red, so the views on the streets and mountains are very attractive. There is a mountain near my house. I love going there to enjoy the autumn leaves.

Closing

느낌 및 의견 For these reasons, I like fall. If you have any plans to visit Korea, fall is the perfect season.

한국의 사계절은 봄, 여름, 가을, 겨울이 뚜렷합니다. 사계절 중에 가장 좋아하는 계절은 가을입니다. 가을은 날씨가 아주 좋고 기온도 적당하기 때문에 공원에 가거나 배드민턴을 치는 등 야외 활동을 하기 좋습니다. 저는 주중에 아내와 종종 야외 활동을 합니다. 또한 가을 경치도 아주 아름답습니다. 가을철 나뭇잎이 녹색에서 노란색이나 붉은색으로 물들면서 거리와 산의 경치가 매력적으로 변합니다. 집 근처에는 산이 있습니다. 가을 단풍을 보러 산에 가고는 합니다. 이런 이유에서 저는 가을을 좋아합니다. 만약 한국을 방문할 계획이 있다면 가을이 가장 완벽한 계절입니다.

고득점 tip!

계절에 따른 활동을 묘사할 때에는 각 계절의 날씨 특징와 관련 지어 구체적으로 답변하는 것이 좋습니다. 계절마다 특색 있게 즐길 수 있는 활동이나 자연환경 변화등을 연관지어 이야기하면 더욱 풍성한 답변이 될 수 있습니다. 이때, 현재시제를 사용하는 것에 주의하세요.

 **Use the expressions in the Skill Up section to develop your sentences.**

— Introduction

— Body

— Closing

OPIc
도전! IM+

UNIT 23

약속

UNIT 23 약속

OPIc 도전! IM+

Learning Objectives

약속을 정하는 방식 또는 약속 변경 및 취소 상황을 설명하고 약속과 관련된 경험에 대해 이야기 할 수 있다.

Frequently Asked Questions

- When you have to schedule an appointment, what steps do you take? How do you make appointments?
- What kind of appointments do you usually make with people?
- Tell me about an experience you had when you were unable to keep an appointment.

Brainstorming

Step 1 Brainstorm key words and expressions about the topic.

Step 2 Use the words and expressions to brainstorm possible questions.

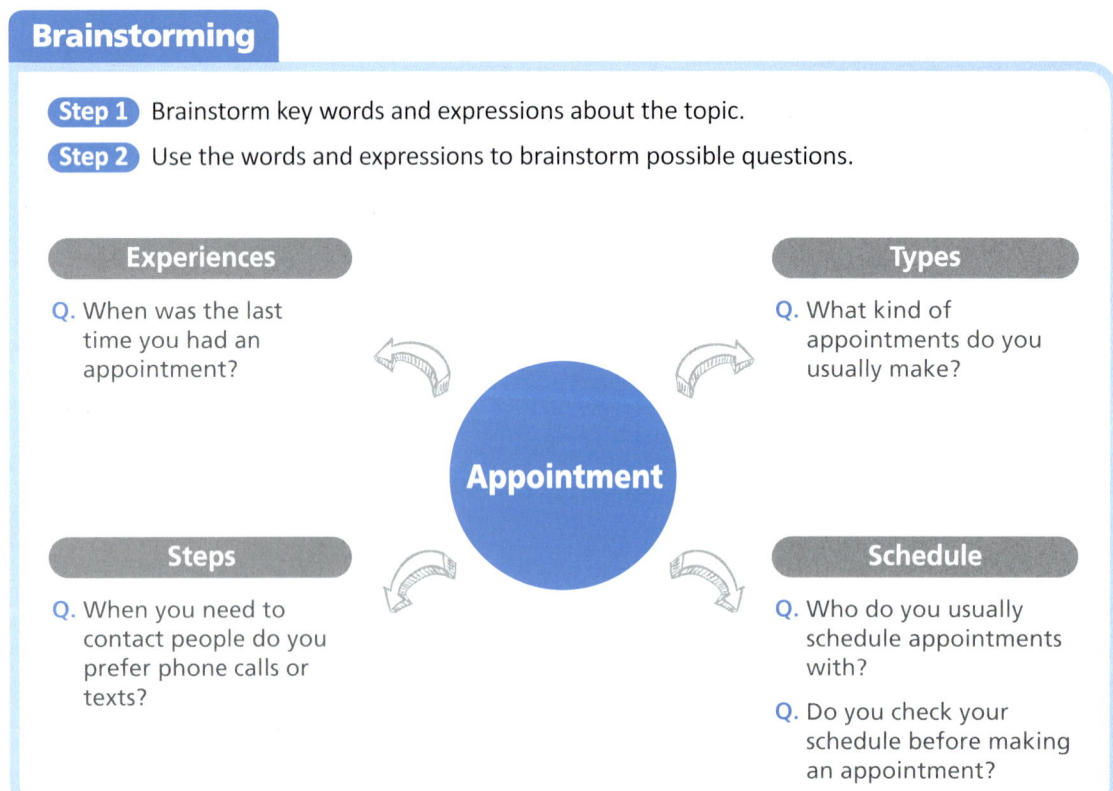

Experiences
Q. When was the last time you had an appointment?

Types
Q. What kind of appointments do you usually make?

Steps
Q. When you need to contact people do you prefer phone calls or texts?

Schedule
Q. Who do you usually schedule appointments with?
Q. Do you check your schedule before making an appointment?

Skill up! Expressions

약속

I usually call to **set up a meeting** with my co-workers.
저는 보통 전화 통화로 동료들과의 회의일정을 정합니다.

I need to **make an appointment** for the dentist.
치과 진료 약속을 잡아야 합니다.

I **frequently have to** make dinner **plans with** my customers.
고객과의 저녁식사 약속을 자주 잡습니다.

I **regularly** have doctor's appointments.
정기적으로 진료 일정을 잡습니다.

I meet up with my friends **once or twice a week**.
일주일에 한두 번 친구들과 만납니다.

약속 잡기

I need to **schedule a meeting** with the project team.
프로젝트 팀과 회의 일정을 잡아야 합니다.

I arrange meetings once in a while.
가끔가다 회의 일정을 조정합니다.

I'll check my hairdresser's schedule.
담당 헤어 디자이너의 일정을 확인할 겁니다.

First, I'll send an e-mail and establish a suitable meeting time.
먼저 이메일을 보내 적당한 회의 시간을 정할 겁니다.

After we set a definite time, I decide on where to meet.
확실한 시간을 정한 후에는 어디에서 만날지를 결정합니다.

I write the appointment in my day planner.
다이어리에 약속 내용을 기입합니다.

When I have a meeting, I **call ahead and confirm the date** to make sure.
회의가 있으면 미리 전화해서 날짜가 맞는지 확인해 둡니다.

Useful Expressions

약속 정하기
check availability
establish a time
call for a time to see
arrange a meeting

즐겨 하는 약속
regularly have a doctor's appointment
meet up with my friends once or twice a week
most of my appointments include

업무 약속을 정할 때의 방식
call and ask for his or her available time
call to check on the time
make sure of the scheduled time
make meeting notes

업무약속 당일
confirm the meeting time a day ahead
get ready for a meeting

약속 변경 및 취소하기
postpone | put off | delay |
hold off | break off | call off |
reschedule | rearrange |
set[suggest] another time

How to Answer

Q1. When you have to schedule an appointment, what steps do you take? How do you make appointments?

내용구성하기	Introduction	☑ 약속을 주로 하는 대상
	Body	☑ 주로 하는 약속 ☑ 약속을 정할 때 고려하는 요소 ☑ 약속 정하는 방식
	Closing	☑ 느낌 및 의견

Introduction

(약속을 주로 하는 대상) Most of my appointments involve meeting with customers.

Body

(주로 하는 약속) I work in sales, so I travel a lot. I often set up meetings several weeks in advance.

(약속을 정할 때 고려하는 요소) It is complex setting up meetings because I want to see several customers in one trip. But people are sometimes not available when I want to see them.

(약속 정하는 방식) To set up appointments, I first e-mail my customers to check their schedules. Then, I call the airline to check flight availability. After that, I confirm my schedule with everyone.

Closing

(느낌 및 의견) Setting up several meetings at once can be complicated.

제 약속 중 대부분은 고객과의 만남입니다. 저는 영업부에서 일하기 때문에 출장을 많이 갑니다. 몇 주 전에 미리 미팅 계획을 잡아 놓습니다. 미팅 일정을 잡는 일은 복잡한데 한번의 출장에서 여러 명의 고객을 만나야 하기 때문입니다. 내가 고객을 보고 싶을 때 상대방은 불가능한 경우도 종종 있습니다. 약속을 잡기 위해서 먼저 고객들에게 일정을 확인하는 이메일을 씁니다. 그런 다음 항공사에 전화해 항공권이 가능한지 확인합니다. 그런 다음 제 일정을 모든 사람과 확인합니다. 한번에 여러 건의 미팅을 잡는 일은 복잡합니다.

답변 tip!

자주 출제되는 돌발 질문 중 한가지는 약속에 관한 것입니다. 주로 일상생활에서의 약속, 회사생활에서의 약속으로 분류하여 생각해볼 수 있습니다. 질문 유형으로는 1) 약속을 정하는 단계(방식), 2) 약속변경 및 취소한 상황 설명하기, 3) 약속과 관련된 경험(가장 최근의 약속) 등이 있습니다.

Q2. What kind of appointments do you make with people?

내용구성하기	Introduction	☑ 주로 약속을 하는 사람들
	Body	☑ 약속 상대
	Closing	☑ 느낌 및 의견

Introduction

주로 약속을 하는 사람들 I make many different kinds of appointments with people. I have meetings with my co-workers, doctor's appointments, hair appointments and so on.

Body

약속 상대① When I want to see a doctor, I first call, check their availability, and make an appointment.

약속 상대② When I arrange meetings with my co-workers, I check everyone's schedule. After that, I set a place and date. I e-mail them to inform them when and where we will meet.

Closing

느낌 및 의견 I don't want to waste my time or others' time, so I always try to keep my appointments.

저는 사람들과 다양한 종류의 약속을 잡습니다. 동료들과의 회의 약속도 있고, 병원 진찰 약속이나, 미용실 약속 등도 있습니다. 의사를 보러 갈 때는 먼저 전화를 해서 진료가 가능한지 확인하고 약속을 잡습니다. 동료들과의 회의 일정을 조정할 때는 모든 인원의 일정을 확인합니다. 그런 다음 장소와 날짜를 정합니다. 이메일로 만나는 장소와 시간을 공지합니다. 내 시간이나 다른 사람의 시간을 낭비하는 것이 싫기 때문에 저는 항상 약속을 지키려고 노력합니다.

고득점 tip!

'약속'의 뜻을 가지고 있지만 혼동하기 쉬운 어휘 사용에 주의합시다.
promise: 무엇인가를 다짐하는 의지의 표현.
appointment: 병원 진료, 일, 회의 등의 특정한 목표를 가지고 있는 시간 약속의 표현.
plan: 친구와의 가벼운 의미의 시간 약속의 표현.

My Answer — Use the expressions in the Skill Up section to develop your sentences.

— Introduction

— Body

— Closing

OPIc
도전! IM+

UNIT 24

쇼핑

UNIT 24 쇼핑

OPIc 도전! IM+

Learning Objectives

자주가는 쇼핑 장소에 대해 소개하고 쇼핑패턴 및 쇼핑경험에 대해 이야기 할 수 있다.

Frequently Asked Questions

- Tell me about your favorite store to shop at. Where is it? Why do you like shopping there?
- When did you go grocery shopping most recently? What did you buy?
- How often do you go shopping? Who do you usually go with? Describe your routine at a shopping mall.
- What do you prefer: online shopping or going to the store? Why?

Brainstorming

Step 1 Brainstorm key words and expressions about the topic.

Step 2 Use the words and expressions to brainstorm possible questions.

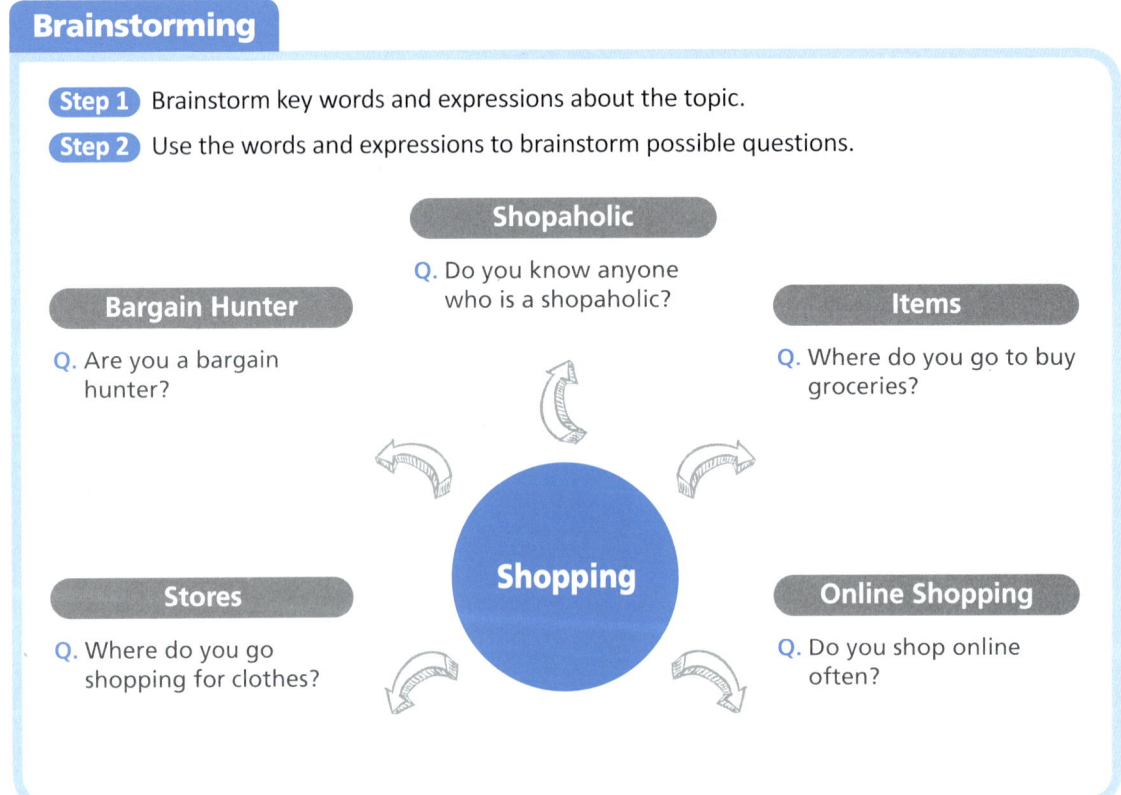

Shopaholic
Q. Do you know anyone who is a shopaholic?

Bargain Hunter
Q. Are you a bargain hunter?

Items
Q. Where do you go to buy groceries?

Stores
Q. Where do you go shopping for clothes?

Online Shopping
Q. Do you shop online often?

Shopping

Skill up! Expressions

쇼핑하기

I often go to **a department store** in town.
동네에 있는 백화점에 자주 갑니다.

I go shopping at **a discount store** near my house for groceries and household items once a week.
일주일에 한번 집 근처에 있는 할인점으로 쇼핑을 가서 먹거리와 생활용품을 삽니다.

I usually go shopping at **a drug and cosmetics store** near my office.
사무실 근처에 있는 화장품 매장에서 보통 쇼핑을 합니다.

I think **underground shopping malls** are the best part of subway stations.
지하 쇼핑몰은 지하철 역의 가장 좋은 점이라고 생각합니다.

I like shopping at the department store near my house because I can get almost anything in one place.
집 근처 백화점에서 쇼핑하는 것을 좋아하는데 한 곳에서 거의 모든 것을 구할 수 있기 때문입니다.

I like shopping at **the local market** in my town because the veggies and fruit are very fresh.
저는 동네의 재래 시장에서 쇼핑하는 것을 좋아하는데 채소와 과일이 매우 신선하기 때문입니다.

Shopping with my wife is one of my favorite weekend activities.
아내와의 쇼핑은 제가 제일 좋아하는 주말 일과 중 하나입니다.

I **buy beer** when I go grocery shopping with my wife.
아내와 장을 보러 가면 저는 맥주를 삽니다.

Some clothes were on sale, so I bought a pair of jeans.
할인하는 옷들이 있길래 청바지를 샀습니다.

I had some difficulties while shopping.
쇼핑하는 동안 약간 문제가 있었습니다.

Two months ago, I bought a pair of shorts from an online store. They were too big and I got a refund.
두 달 전 온라인으로 반바지를 샀었습니다. 그런데 옷이 너무 커서 환불을 받았습니다.

People were packed in the mall like sardines.
통조림 속 정어리처럼 쇼핑몰에 사람들이 바글바글했습니다.

Useful Expressions

쇼핑 장소
underground shopping arcade
grocery store
electronics plaza
outlet mall
online shopping mall
street vendor

물건을 구입할 때 고려사항
buy practical items
look for bargains
shop for the best price
look for quality items

쇼핑 전 후에 하는 일
ask for an opinion about the item
search for shopping information on the Internet
check the product reviews
look through brochures
grab a bite at the food court

쇼핑 활동
browse around the shop
bargain [haggle] over the price
check the price tag
consider other options

지불방법 및 그에 대한 이유
pay with my cash card
use gift cards
stick to a budget
watch what I spend
limit my spending

How to Answer

Q1. Tell me about your favorite store to shop at. Where is it? Why do you like shopping there?

내용구성하기		
	Introduction	☑ 자주가는 쇼핑 장소
	Body	☑ 그 상점을 좋아하는 이유 ☑ 상점 묘사 ☑ 상점에서 할 수 있는 다른 활동
	Closing	☑ 느낌 및 의견

Introduction
자주가는 쇼핑 장소 I will tell you about my favorite place to go shopping. I like shopping at a department store near my house called AK.

Body
그 상점을 좋아하는 이유 I often go there with my wife. Actually, it's my wife's favorite place. We go shopping there because we can find almost anything in one place.

상점 묘사 On the 1st floor, there are many clothing stores and cosmetic stores. My wife usually spends one or two hours there. My favorite place is the store selling sports items on the 2nd floor. Also, it has many different facilities.

상점에서 할 수 있는 다른 활동 So before or after shopping, we can do other activities, like watch movies or drink coffee.

Closing
느낌 및 의견 Sometimes, I shop online and go to other stores but my favorite place to go shopping is the department store.

가장 좋아하는 쇼핑 장소에 대해 이야기해보겠습니다. 저는 집 근처에 있는 AK백화점에서 쇼핑하는 것을 좋아합니다. 저는 아내와 함께 그곳에 자주 갑니다. 사실 그곳은 아내가 가장 좋아하는 곳입니다. 그곳에서 쇼핑하는 이유는 거의 모든 것을 한 장소에서 찾을 수 있기 때문입니다. 1층에는 많은 의류 및 화장품 코너가 있습니다. 아내는 보통 그곳에서 한두 시간을 보냅니다. 제가 가장 좋아하는 장소는 2층에 있는 스포츠 용품 판매점입니다. 또한 다양한 시설을 많이 갖추고 있어 쇼핑 전이나 후에 영화를 보거나 커피를 마시는 등 다른 활동도 할 수 있습니다. 때로는 온라인으로 쇼핑을 하고 다른 상점에 갈 때도 있지만, 제가 가장 좋아하는 쇼핑 장소는 백화점입니다.

답변 tip!

뉴오픽이 도입되면서 자주 출제되는 돌발문제입니다. 쇼핑과 관련해서는 1) 쇼핑패턴(누구와 언제, 어디에서, 얼마나 자주 쇼핑을 하는지), 2) 쇼핑경험 (비용지불 방법 및 환불 경험/ 쇼핑 방식 및 활동), 3) 쇼핑 장소에 대한 묘사 등에 대한 질문들이 출제됩니다. 기본적으로 쇼핑습관 및 구매활동에 대한 답변을 구성해 돌발 상황을 대비해 두는 것이 좋습니다.

Q2. When did you go grocery shopping most recently? What did you buy?

내용구성하기		
Introduction	☑ 최근 쇼핑 경험	
Body	☑ 같이 간 사람　☑ 구입한 물건　☑ 쇼핑 후 한 일	
Closing	☑ 느낌 및 의견	

Introduction
[최근 쇼핑 경험] I went grocery shopping last weekend with my family at a discount store called Emart.

Body
[같이 간 사람 & 구입한 물건] As I mentioned before, I have 3 sons. It's not really easy to go grocery shopping with them. My sons always want to buy sweets and snacks and my wife always wants wine. Last weekend, I went shopping and bought vegetables, meat, fruit, chips, and some chocolate for my kids and 5 bottles of wine for my wife.

[쇼핑 후 한 일] After shopping, we went to a buffet on the 3rd floor of the store.

Closing
[느낌 및 의견] Yes, shopping together is a bit tough but I still love the time with my family.

저는 지난 주에 가족과 이마트라는 할인점에서 장을 봤습니다. 앞서 말씀 드렸듯이 저에겐 세 명의 아들이 있습니다. 아이들과 함께 장을 본다는 건 정말 쉬운 일이 아니죠. 아들들은 항상 사탕이나 간식을 사고 싶어 하고 아내는 와인을 사고 싶어 합니다. 지난 주말에는 쇼핑할 때, 야채, 고기, 과일, 과자와 아이들이 먹을 초콜릿을 사고 아내는 와인을 5병을 샀습니다. 쇼핑 후에는 건물 3층에 있는 뷔페에 갔습니다. 맞아요, 다 함께 쇼핑한다는 건 힘든 일이지만 가족과 함께하는 시간은 여전히 소중합니다.

고득점 tip!
쇼핑을 할 때 주로 어떤 물건을 구입하는지 나열하는 것도 좋지만 쇼핑 후 어떤 활동을 하는지도 함께 묘사하면 풍성한 답변이 될 수 있습니다. 평소 쇼핑을 좋아하지 않는다면 마트에서 식료품 구매나 좋아하는 게임, 게임 아이템 구매 등으로 확장해서 답변을 구성할 수 있습니다.

My Answer — Use the expressions in the Skill Up section to develop your sentences.

— Introduction

— Body

— Closing

실전 OPIc

☑ Actual Test 1
☑ Actual Test 2

ACTUAL TEST 1

Q1 Tell me about yourself and what you usually do on the weekends.

Q2 Describe the geography of your country. Are there mountains? Is the seashore part of the geography? Are there lakes? Discuss all the details you can about the geography and landscape in your country.

Q3 I would like to know about a region that is geographically special. Where is it? Why is it special? Tell me about it in as much detail as possible.

Q4 Have you ever been to a place that is geographically unique or special? Where was it? Why did you visit there? What did you see?

Q5 You said in the survey that you enjoy going to a park. I would like to know about a park that you usually go to. What is the name of the park? Why is it so special to you? What can you see there? Tell me about the park in as much detail as possible.

Q6 What do you usually do at the park? What kind of activities do you usually do? Who do you do the activities with? Tell me about your routine when you go to the park.

Q7 When was the last time you visited the park? When was it? Where did you go? What happened? Were you with anyone else? Please tell me everything about it.

Q8 Tell me about a healthy person you know. What does he or she look like? What kind of food does he or she like to eat? How did you meet him or her?

Q9 If you wanted to be a healthy person, how would you spend your daily life? What type of activities would you have to do? What kind of food would you need to eat? Tell me in as much detail as possible.

Q10 Have you ever done anything to be a healthy person? What did you do? What did you eat? Tell me your experience in as much detail as possible.

Q11 I will give you a situation to act out. You are planning to travel and would like to rent a car. Call a rental car agency and ask 3 or 4 questions about renting a car.

Q12 I am afraid that there is a problem that you need to resolve. Your travel agency called and told you that your trip has been cancelled. Call your friend, explain the situation, and offer 2 or 3 alternatives.

Q13 Have you ever had any difficulties planning a trip? When was it? Where did you want to go? What happened? How did you resolve the situation? Tell me about it from the beginning to the end.

Q14 I would like to know what you think the differences between Korean dishes and dishes from other countries are. Are there any similarities? Compare the dishes in as much detail as possible.

Q15 Have you heard about any issues related to water or food shortages around the world? Tell me your opinion about these issues in detail.

ACTUAL TEST 2

Q1 Tell me about yourself and what you usually do on the weekends.

Q2 You indicated that you like to listen to music. What type of music do you like? When and how often do you enjoy them? Who do you like to listen to? Why do you like them?

Q3 When did you first become interested in music? Did anyone influence your musical preferences? Do you still listen to the same kind of music you did when you were a child? If not, how have your preferences changed?

Q4 Do you have any unexpected or special memories from when you went to a concert? Whose concert was it? When did you go? What happened? Why was it so special to you? Explain your experience in detail.

Q5 Could you tell me about the banks in your country? When do they open and close? What do they look like? Where are they located? Also, please describe the people who work at a bank.

Q6 Could you describe how banks in your country have changed over time? Do you think they have improved? Please describe the differences between banks of the past and those of the present in as much detail as possible.

Q7 Please tell me about the last time you went to a bank. Which bank did you go to? Why did you choose that bank? When was it? How long did your visit take? Tell me about everything in detail.

Q8 I would like to know about your house. What does it look like? Describe your room. What can you see there? Tell about your house and your room in detail.

Q9 I would like you to tell me about the house you are currently living in and then compare it to a house you lived in before. What are some differences? Are those differences better or worse? Please compare the two houses in as much detail as possible.

Q10 Have you ever done anything special at home? What did you do? Tell me about your experience in as much detail as possible.

Q11 I'll give you a certain situation to act out. Let's assume that you have a toothache. Call the dentist's office and ask 3 or 4 questions to make an appointment.

Q12 I'm afraid that there is a problem you have to solve. You are supposed to go to the dentist tomorrow. But you cannot keep the appointment and you can only go there next week. Call the dentist's office, explain the situation and give a few alternatives.

Q13 Have you cancelled or delayed an important appointment? Why did you do so? How did you resolve the situation?

Q14 What are some differences between a trip you took in the past and one that you might take in the present? Please describe the differences in detail.

Q15 Experts say it is important to have a vacation. Do you agree or disagree? What are your reasons? I would like you to tell me in as much detail as possible.

OPIc
도전! IM+

IV

부록

IM-IH 학습가이드

Strategies for Progressing from Intermediate Mid to Intermediate High

Intermediate Mid (IM)	Intermediate High (IH)
A rating of Intermediate Mid indicates that the Speaker is able to: • fulfill all of the requirements for the Intermediate level (creates with language by asking and answering questions about familiar topics, in sentences and strings of sentences). • produce Intermediate level responses with both quantity and quality. • produce responses that are consistently strong across all the Intermediate level assessment criteria.	A rating of Intermediate High indicates that the Speaker is: • able to demonstrate the ability to function at the Advanced level most of the time. • unable to sustain Advanced-level across <u>all rating criteria</u> all of the time.
Intermediate Mid speakers are at ease when performing Intermediate-level tasks and do so with significant quality and quantity of Intermediate language. They are able to express themselves by creating with the language, in part by combining and recombining known elements and conversational input to produce responses typically consisting of sentences and strings of sentences. Their speech may contain pauses, reformulations, and self-corrections as they search for adequate vocabulary and appropriate language forms to express themselves. In spite of the possible limitations in their vocabulary, pronunciation, and syntax, they are generally understood by sympathetic interlocutors accustomed to dealing with non-natives.	**Intermediate High** speakers operate at the advanced level most of the time, but have breakdown in one or more features of the Advanced level. Breakdown can be, among other things, failure to perform the required functions of the Advanced level, inability to maintain the appropriate time frame when narrating and/or describing about past/future (for example, reverting to present when talking about the past); failure to speak consistently in paragraph form when required by the function; or issues with accuracy so that the message becomes confusing for listeners (this may include weaknesses in pronunciation).

Strategies for Progressing from Intermediate Mid to Intermediate High
(Note: A speaker at Intermediate Mid should start focusing on developing Advanced-level language. The Intermediate High rating indicates that a speaker is functioning at the Advanced level, but not all of the time. The strategies for progressing to IH will be similar to the strategies for progressing to A.)

1. Tell stories. Be sure to tell the whole story from beginning to end. Use words and phrases that support the chronology of your story. With a conversational partner, practice explaining and/or clarifying specific narrations and descriptions so that the listener is not in any way confused about the chronology of events.

2. Use appropriate verb forms to maintain descriptions and narrations in past, present, and future time.

3. Do not avoid situations in which you must resolve a situation with an unexpected turn of events (e.g. a lost wallet, a missed airplane, locked door, etc.) Role play practice is particularly helpful in developing strategies to "think on your feet."

4. Use connecting words (and, but, also, however, first, next, in addition, etc.) within and between sentences to produce oral paragraphs. These connectors (and others) can help you to develop greater clarity, organization, and detail in your speech.

5. Talk about familiar people, places, objects, buildings, cities, etc. using as much language as you can. Elaborate by including as much detail as you can. Use dependent clauses to add richness to your descriptions. Describe in a way that "paints a picture" for the listener.

6. Keep a written journal in which you record interesting observations, events, both personal and of a more general nature (e.g., current events in your community, city, country, etc.) Identify new vocabulary and phrases that are necessary to talk about these events. First write notes about the events, then practice telling them to a conversational partner while only referring to your notes, and ultimately doing so without using your notes at all.

7. Increase exposure to target language media (news broadcasts constitute excellent examples of narrations and descriptions in the past). Talk about what you have heard about reported on the radio or TV.

8. Read newspapers, magazines, and books in the target language. Retell events you have read about and that are of general interest.

9. If possible, participate in immersion experiences in English at home or abroad. The more "time on task," performing real-world functions across a variety of contexts in the language, the more likely you will achieve Advanced-level proficiency.

10. Work with a conversation partner or tutor who is familiar with your proficiency goals and the criteria for the Advanced level of speaking proficiency. Your conversation partner should provide opportunities for you to speak extemporaneously. Keep in mind that Advanced level speech is that which is produced by a full conversational partner. It is not rehearsed or prepared speech.

11. Work to improve pronunciation and intonation so that you can be understood by speakers of English who are not accustomed to interacting with learners.

12. Work to improve pronunciation and intonation so that you can be understood by other speakers of the language who are not accustomed to interacting with learners.

OPIc 가이드 라인

American Council on the Teaching of Foreign Languages Oral Proficiency Ratings*
Brief Summary of OPIc Ratings(NH to A)
American Council on the Teaching of Foreign Languages

Novice High (NH)

A rating of Novice High indicates that the Speaker is:

- able to demonstrate the ability to function at the Intermediate level most of the time.
- unable to sustain Intermediate level across <u>all rating criteria</u> all of the time.

Novice High speakers operate at the Intermediate level most of the time, but have breakdown in one or more features of the Intermediate level. Breakdown can be, among other things, failure to perform the required functions of the Intermediate level, such as the inability to create with the language (make their own personalized meaning) across a limited range of everyday topics; failure to use simple sentences consistently when required by the function; or issues with pronunciation and accuracy so that the message becomes confusing for listeners.

Intermediate Low (IL)

A rating of Intermediate Low indicates that the Speaker is able to:

- fulfill all of the requirements for the Intermediate level (creates with language by asking and answering questions about familiar topics, in sentences and strings of sentences).
- produce Intermediate level responses but struggles to do so
- communicate primarily by using what they have practiced and hear from their interlocutors.

Intermediate Low speakers are able to perform Intermediate-level tasks, albeit barely. They are able to express themselves by creating with the language, primarily by combining and recombining known elements (what they have learned) and conversational input to produce responses typically consisting of short, discrete sentences. Their responses are often filled with hesitancy and inaccuracies as they search for the appropriate vocabulary and linguistic forms. Their speech is characterized by frequent pauses. Their language, including pronunciation, is strongly influenced by their first language, and therefore can generally be understood by sympathetic interlocutors, especially those accustomed to dealing with learners.

Intermediate Mid (IM)

A rating of Intermediate Mid indicates that the Speaker is able to:

- fulfill all of the requirements for the Intermediate level (creates with language by asking and answering questions about familiar topics, in sentences and strings of sentences).
- produce Intermediate level responses with both quantity and quality.
- produce responses that are consistently strong across all the Intermediate level assessment criteria.

Intermediate Mid speakers are at ease when performing Intermediate-level tasks and do so with significant quality and quantity of Intermediate language. They are able to express themselves by creating with the language, in part by combining and recombining known elements and conversational input to produce responses typically consisting of sentences and strings of sentences. Their speech may contain pauses, reformulations, and self-corrections as they search for adequate vocabulary and appropriate language forms to express themselves. In spite of the possible limitations in their vocabulary, pronunciation, and syntax, they are generally understood by sympathetic interlocutors accustomed to dealing with non-natives.

Intermediate High (IH)

A rating of Intermediate High indicates that the Speaker is:

- able to demonstrate the ability to function at the Advanced level most of the time.
- unable to sustain Advanced-level across <u>all rating criteria</u> all of the time.

Intermediate High speakers operate at the advanced level most of the time, but have breakdown in one or more features of the Advanced level. Breakdown can be, among other things, failure to perform the required functions of the Advanced level, inability to maintain the appropriate time frame when narrating and/or describing about past/future (for example, reverting to present when talking about the past); failure to speak consistently in paragraph form when required by the function; or issues with accuracy so that the message becomes confusing for listeners (this may include weaknesses in pronunciation).

Advanced (A)

A rating of Advanced indicates that the Speakers is able to:

- narrate and describe in all major time frames in order to have conversations about both personal experiences, as well as topics related to community interest.
- handle a routine situation with an unexpected complication.
- produce paragraph-length or connected discourse when narrating and describing about a variety of topics.
- esolve a routine social transaction with an unanticipated complication.

Advanced-level speakers are consistently understood by native speakers who have no experience dealing with non-native speakers of the language being assessed. In other words, their message does not become lost, though this may occasionally require repetition or restatement.

OPIc 금지답변

The OPIc is a test of spoken language proficiency. Proficiency is defined as the ability to use spoken language for real world purposes in order to engage in a spontaneous communicative exchange. Using recited responses during an OPIc does not provide sufficient evidence of language proficiency for a rater to assign an ACTFL proficiency rating. Recited responses are defined as entire passages that have been scripted, memorized and then reproduced during the OPIc.

The OPIc is rated by human raters who are trained to listen for patterns of strengths and patterns of weakness. The language you produce throughout the test is rated holistically according to the ACTFL Proficiency Guidelines 2012 – Speaking. Raters expect to hear personalized responses that address both the topic and the question asked. Raters do not expect perfection at any level. They recognize that as one is learning a language, spontaneous responses may contain imperfections and irregularities.

OPIc raters are also trained to recognize language that is pre-scripted and recited from memory during the test. The use of scripted responses that are recited from memory will negatively impact your rating.

What does it mean to be rated Novice High for recited memorized responses? Consistent use of memorized material is a function of the Novice level. If you wish to receive a rating above Novice, you must demonstrate the ability to communicate on a range of topics in your own words. You must create with the language in order to participate in genuine communicative conversations. If you consistently recite responses that have been memorized ahead of time, the highest rating you are likely to receive is Novice High. This indicates that your speech sample contains much language that has been memorized and recalled.

Below are indicators that raters will recognize as recited, memorized responses.

A speaker may:

- Recite responses that are in wide circulation. Raters hear the same response repeated by hundreds of test-takers. This signals the rater that you are reciting responses that are not your own, and therefore may not be able to engage in actual interpersonal conversations. Recent examples include stories about the following:
  - Twisted ankle
  - Spilled coffee on white pants
  - Changing wallpaper that had mold on it, the project takes a half a day
  - Interest in music, you usually like ballads, but sometimes you like to listen to upbeat music when working out or driving
  - Coming upon a concert on the beach with Psy and others who all did their signature numbers
  - Running into someone while on the phone, who later becomes your boyfriend/girlfriend/spouse
  - Living in a house with a garden as a child, but now you have to be considerate of your neighbors because you live in an apartment
  - Getting locked in the bathroom, at home or on vacation
  - Having the computer freeze while working on an important paper that is due in one hour
  - Spending time at home on your last vacation, first with family, then meeting old friends from school, one of them is getting married; you also did some soul searching and thought about your career and future
  - Placing an online order that didn't arrive
  - Recycling as a community event; getting candy as a child from the person collecting recycling
  - Borrowing a friend's wireless mouse that broke
- Repeat the exact same answer or substantial parts of it in response to more than one prompt.
- Provide a response that is not related to the question.
- Provide a response that is related to a different OPIc prompt that may or may not even occur in that particular test.
- Perform a Role Play situation that was not asked for, or pretend to be in a Role Play situation when the question does not call for it.

Reminder to OPIc Test-Takers

You want to show your spoken language ability at its best. In order to do so, express your own meaning using spontaneous language when responding to OPIc prompts. Address the topic and question that is asked. Remember that reciting scripted responses will result in a Novice-level rating.